Legal frameworks for eHealth

Based on the findings of the second global survey on eHealth

Global Observatory for eHealth series - Volume 5

Acknowledgments

This report would not have been possible without the input of the Observatory's extensive network of eHealth experts and the support of numerous colleagues at the World Health Organization headquarters, regional, and country offices. Sincere thanks are due to over 800 eHealth experts in 114 countries worldwide who assisted with the design, implementation, and completion of the second global survey.

Special thanks to the author of this work Petra Wilson, and the expert reviewers including: Najeeb Al Shorbaji, Isabelle Andoulsi, George Crooks, Joan Dzenowagis, Carlisle George, and Maurice Mars. Renata Pieratti provided research support on aspects of Brazilian law.

We are grateful to the Rockefeller Foundation for its financial support and to the European Commission Directorate General for the Information Society and Media for the publication of the report.

Our appreciation goes to Jillian Reichenbach Ott for the design and layout, Kai Lashley for editing and Rebecca Gordon for proof reading.

The global survey and this report were prepared and managed by the WHO Global Observatory for eHealth: Misha Kay, Jonathan Santos, and Marina Takane.

Photo credits: ©Thinkstock.

Table of contents

Executive summary 5

1. Introduction 9

   1.1 Is privacy a culturally dependant concept? 9

   1.2 Is respect for privacy important in the uptake of eHealth? . . 12

   1.3 Privacy or confidentiality of EHRs - a note on terminology . . 15

2. The ethical and legal aspects of privacy in health care:
   a literature review 17

   2.1 Privacy of health related information as an ethical concept . 18

   2.2 The protection of privacy of health related information
       through law 21

   2.3 Binding international law on privacy of health related information 23

       The Universal Declaration of Human Rights 23
       The European Convention on Human Rights 23
       European Union Directive on the protection of individuals with regard to the
       processing of personal data and on the free movement of such data 25

   2.4 International non-binding agreements 28

       Convention for the Protection of Individuals with regard to
       Automatic Processing of Personal Data 28
       Council of Europe Recommendation No. R (97) 5 on the
       protection of medical data 28
       WHO: A Declaration on the Promotion of Patients' Rights in Europe . . . 29

   2.5 National law on privacy of health related information . . 30

       Use of EHRs in Brazil 33
       Legislative responses to EHRs in the USA 34

3. Analysis of survey results   37

3.1. General privacy legislation   38
Results 38
Discussion 40

3.2 EHR privacy legislation   42
Results 42
Discussion 45

3.3 Legislation to regulate the sharing of health related data for patient care.   46
Results 47
Discussion 53

3.4 Legislation on patient access and the control of EHRs   55
Results 56
Discussion 60

3.5 EHRs for research   61
Results 62
Discussion 63

4. Conclusions   65

4.1 Building trust   67

4.2 Making data work: expanding the uses of EHRs   68

5. References   71

6. Appendix 1. Methodology of the second global survey on eHealth — 75

Purpose — 75
Survey implementation — 76
Survey instrument — 76
Survey development — 78
Data Collector — 78
Preparation to launch the survey — 79
Survey — 80
Limitations — 80
Data processing — 81
Response rate — 82
Response rate by WHO region — 83
Response rate by World Bank income group — 84
References — 84

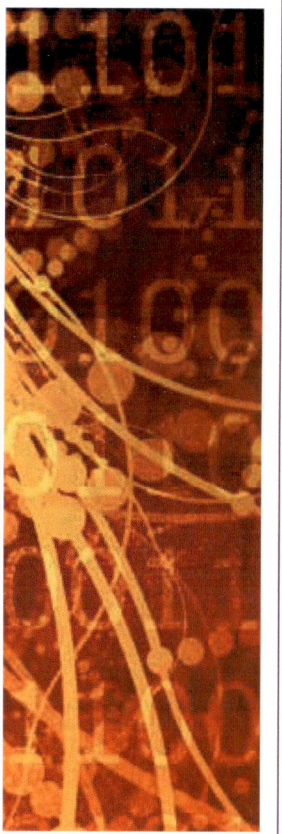

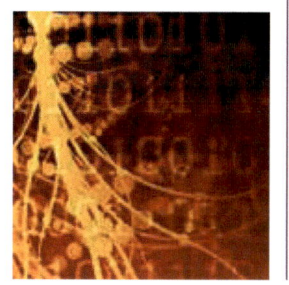

Executive summary

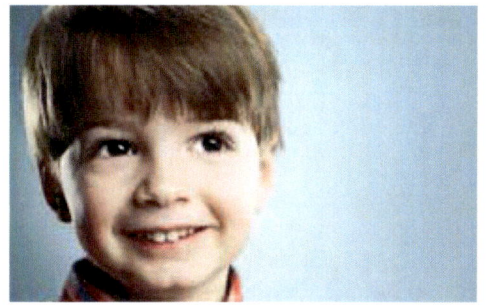 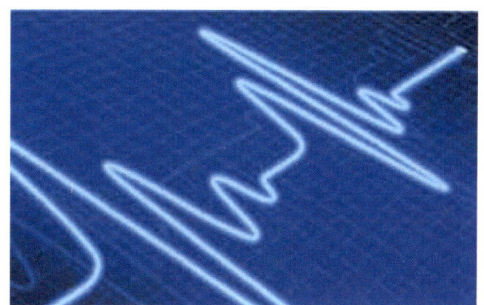 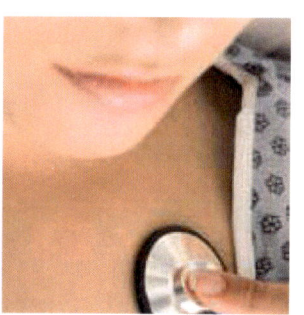

Given that privacy of the doctor-patient relationship is at the heart of good health care, and that the electronic health record (EHR) is at the heart of good eHealth practice, the question arises: Is privacy legislation at the heart of the EHR? The second global survey on eHealth conducted by the Global Observatory for eHealth (GOe) set out to answer that question by investigating the extent to which the legal frameworks in the Member States of the World Health Organization (WHO) address the need to protect patient privacy in EHRs as health care systems move towards leveraging the power of EHRs to deliver safer, more efficient, and more accessible health care.

The survey began with a question on the existence of generic privacy legislation followed by questions to establish if specific rules had been adopted to address privacy in EHRs. A series of questions followed pertaining to the way in which privacy is addressed in transmittable EHRs and patients' rights to access, correct, and control the use of the EHR. The investigation ended by broaching the issue of privacy protection in secondary uses of data contained in EHRs, such as for international research purposes.

In the present report the analysis of the survey responses is preceded by an overview of the ethical and legal roots of privacy protection. Focusing on the ethical concepts of autonomy, beneficence, and justice, the report reminds the reader of the early recognition of the duty of privacy in the Hippocratic Oath and goes on to consider how that is reflected in international binding legislation such as the United Nations Declaration on Human Rights and the European Union Data Protection Directive, as well as non-binding international codes of practice.

It is important to note that the survey asked questions specifically about protecting privacy in EHRs, it did not cover other areas of legislation which have a significant impact on adoption of EHRs and how they are used. Therefore this report does not discuss the impact of technology to drive unique citizen identification, nor the legislation adopted to support it. It goes without saying however that as such technology is adopted for patient identification purposes, it will have a significant impact on the acceptance of EHRs and the protection of privacy in their use.

Survey results show that a generally sound base of generic privacy protection exists: some 70% of the 113 responding countries reported having legislation providing a basic right to privacy, and the remaining 30% anticipate that such legislation would be adopted by 2015. When reviewing the existence of legislation specifically protecting the privacy of the EHR these values are reversed, however: only 30% globally reported having such legislation in place. Further analysis of the responses on the use of legislation to ensure privacy in sharing EHRs for treatment or research purposes reveals that very few countries have established comprehensive legal frameworks on EHRs (e.g. only 10% of countries reported having legislation which covers cross-border EHR sharing).

Such privacy legislation is found mainly in developed countries. It may be therefore that as developing countries adopt more eHealth solutions a new perspective on EHR privacy will emerge, which reflects local cultural norms and a legal environment for the protection of privacy in health care that diverges from the European and American norms highlighted in this report. While this may affect the detailed interpretation of EHR privacy and its execution through legislation, the fact that developing countries already showed a very good level of recognition of the basic concept of privacy, indicates that while culture may give legal protection of privacy a different value in different regions, the core concept is well understood globally.

The fact that legislation specifically addressing EHR privacy exists predominantly in countries where a considerable investment in eHealth has already been made, would seem to indicate that legislation is being developed reactively once policies to deploy eHealth have been adopted. The power of law to act as a catalyst and facilitator to drive eHealth adoption is therefore not being leveraged in Member States. While this may have relatively limited side-effects when eHealth is being used primarily as a standalone solution in one health care institution, it will significantly impact the potential of using valuable eHealth tools such as EHRs across organizations or countries.

The ability to make wide use of EHRs and other eHealth tools will become increasingly important in both developed and developing countries. In the former, EHRs and related eHealth tools will play a key role of providing health care to ageing populations in which social care and health care need to be much more closely connected and where capacity demands will require that care is delivered outside traditional settings such as hospitals. The protection of privacy will also be a significant issue in supporting the changing nature of health care in developing countries, in which mobile eHealth solutions are emerging as an integral part of the health care infrastructure, as demonstrated in the publication *mHealth: new horizons for health through mobile technologies.*

While protection of privacy is of course only one of a number of legal issues that has to be addressed in eHealth, it is a good indicator of the extent to which wider legal issues in eHealth are being addressed at national and international levels. It also provides an answer to the question: Is privacy at the heart of the EHR? The answer would seem to be yes, but only a qualified yes. To date the use of law has not extended beyond simple privacy protection in many countries, with only a few adopting legislation to facilitate appropriate sharing of EHR data and even fewer adopting legislation to support patients' more nuanced interests in data such as a right to correction or deletion. It may be suggested therefore that at present the legislative heart is beating weakly and is failing to pump the power of law to the wider reaches of EHR use to enable health care systems to gain the full benefit of a shareable, accessible, and protected EHR.

1 Introduction

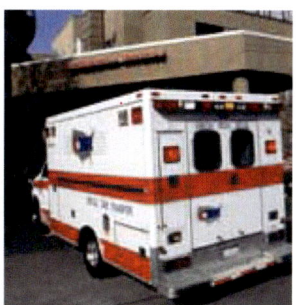

Based on the belief that patient privacy is a core element of good health care practice, and that legislation is a key tool in protecting privacy (1), section six of the second global survey on eHealth conducted by the Global Observatory for eHealth (GOe) focused specifically on the way in which privacy of the electronic health record (EHR) is addressed through legal and regulatory tools. The survey asked a series of questions about the nature of the regulation of privacy in health care and eHealth, in order to ascertain if the regulatory environment was ready for a full and effective exploitation of eHealth solutions.

1.1 Is privacy a culturally dependant concept?

In discussing the concept of privacy, it is worth first noting that the responses to the second global survey on eHealth came from a diverse range of experts representing many different patient groups, health care systems and legal frameworks, which in turn represent some 80% of the world's population. Given the wide cultural perspective of the respondents, it is useful to begin this report with a short overview of the literature on the role of culture in understanding privacy, before examining the responses to the survey on the protection of patient privacy in detail.

The literature shows that any discussion of privacy across nations and cultures must be sensitive to the impact of cultural norms and environments before applying universal concepts of privacy (2–4). This requires not only sensitivity to the local norms within which privacy is being examined, but also awareness of the relevant historical context. Lu (5), looking at recent changes in the understanding of privacy in China, argues that relatively recent changes in political and social structure mean that *people no longer regard individual interests, individual freedom, and individual rights as taboo topics of discussion. In contrast with the not-so-distant past, individual independence and subjectivity have obviously been promoted in their importance and value in social life. Increasing diversity in contemporary Chinese society also makes for greater variety in Chinese ideas of privacy. More and more Chinese citizens begin to give importance to privacy and express concern over protecting emerging rights to privacy (5).*

He maintains therefore that one cannot interpret older Chinese norms of privacy as applying in the same way today as they did one or two generations ago. In the survey the existence of privacy legislation is taken as a baseline indicator of a commonly understandable concept of privacy. However it should be determined, before proceeding, to what extent the existence of privacy legislation is a good indicator of a respect for privacy. It may be that the cultural specificity of the country in which the legislation has been adopted means that not all enactments of privacy legislation can be seen as equal. Orito and Murata *(6)* have, for example, cautioned against interpreting the existence of the Japanese Act for Protection of Personal Data (2005) as a clear indication that Japan has a western style approach to privacy. They argue that the enactment of this legislation should not be seen as a valorization of the concept of privacy in Japan, but rather as a reflection of the external pressures exerted by the international community. Explicitly Orito and Murata cite the influence of the European Data Protection Directive (Directive 95/46/EC) which requires that European Union (EU) Member States only exchange person identifiable data with nations in which regulations on protection of personal data exist (and in which the level of personal data protection is considered adequate). Economic expediency of promoting trade with Europe was therefore the driver of the Japanese legislation, argue Orito and Murata, not a fundamental respect of the value of privacy *(6)*.

Does that mean then, in the context of the survey, that the existence of privacy protection legislation is not a good baseline indicator? Collste *(7)* would argue against such a proposition. In deconstructing arguments such as those made by Orito and Murata he finds that despite differences in the expression of privacy, there is not a deep cultural disagreement concerning the right to privacy. He argues that the concept of privacy is based on three universal intrinsic values: autonomy, freedom, and personal relationships. According to Collste, a respect for these three universal values is in itself a respect for privacy, since privacy is a necessary pre-condition for achieving these values. Although societies and cultures might differ as to what degree privacy is seen as a mean to achieve some of these values, the differences do not mirror a deep cultural difference in the concept of privacy in itself *(7)*.

It would seem therefore that the first question on legal and ethical issues in eHealth in the survey, which asks respondents to clarify if any general laws on protection of privacy exist, provides a good baseline indicator for the respect of privacy. It is accepted however that neither the existence nor the absence of such legislation is a definitive answer to questions of respect for privacy in eHealth. Indeed, the discussion of the survey results will show that even countries which have no generic privacy protection in law may nonetheless use legal mechanisms to protect the privacy of an individual's sensitive health related information; while others with well-established generic privacy legislation may have limited success in translating it into rules which specifically protect privacy of health related data.

As the survey asked specifically about privacy legislation, it is unlikely that many respondents extrapolated out to include related areas of legislation which may protect privacy, but where that is not the specific purpose of the legislation. Thus the responses from India did not make reference to the new initiative on Unique Electronic Identifiers (Aadhaar) which will have a significant impact on allowing healthcare providers to ensure that only eligible people see EHRs, but where that was not a specific objective of the legislation on the adoption of Aadhaar.

It should also be noted that privacy may have quite different resonances in different regions of the world. Commentators have noted that in lower-income countries policy-makers may perceive privacy protection as a luxury that is outweighed by more pressing demands. Indeed, the lower-income countries responding to the survey reported a much less developed range of EHR privacy legislation, and as a result much of the discussion in this report is based on constructions of privacy in higher-income countries.

Furthermore, it is accepted that simply asking about the existence of privacy legislation does not allow a thorough analysis of the nuances of the interpretation of the right to privacy in an EHR, which may vary quite considerably between WHO Member States notwithstanding that they report the existence of such legislation. Therefore, while the question on the existence of privacy legislation must be interpreted with a high degree of cultural sensitivity, it is a useful starting point in assessing the maturity of a country's approach to embracing the new demands of the information society in which, as Giddens *(8)* argues, the "disembedding" of social systems places many new ethical demands on societies. Giddens' thesis on the impact of taking social relations from local contexts of interaction and understanding them within the infinite spans of time-space that modern information and communication technologies (ICTs) allow, provides a useful framework for understanding the nature of privacy in cross-cultural contexts *(9)*. It is therefore in this spirit that a respect for privacy is seen as a core element for allowing the disembedding of traditional face-to-face health care delivery which eHealth is seeking to facilitate.

1.2 Is respect for privacy important in the uptake of eHealth?

The premise underlying the existence of the GOe is that eHealth is an important tool in establishing safe, efficient, and sustainable health care delivery around the world. Thus WHO seeks to encourage the uptake of eHealth as appropriate to a nation's needs and capacities. One reason for this is that projected figures of demographic change show that the dependency ratio between those of traditional working age and retirement age is predicted to drop to a ratio of two working age persons to every one retired-age person in many countries by as soon as 2040 *(10)*.[1] Many WHO regions, in particular the European, Americas and Eastern Mediterranean, have already invested heavily in eHealth solutions to meet the challenges of ageing populations, and are beginning to embrace the idea that in order to meet health care needs in the context of demographic change, a paradigm shift towards more patient-centred care delivered outside the traditional hospital or general practitioner (GP) office environment will have to occur *(11, 12)*.

However, in order for eHealth tools to be truly integrated into daily health and care services, many political and policy changes will have to be made. At the forefront of these changes is of course financial support – while eHealth is the province essentially of those who can pay, it will do little to ease the burden of public health systems in developed and less developed regions. Alongside the many other needs that have been discussed in the Global Observatory for eHealth series, a change in the legal context for health care provision is also necessary, because such systems will have to be able to accommodate secure transfer of information between health facilities and patients' homes and a range of stakeholders in the public, private, and international sectors *(13)*.

The need for development of appropriate legal frameworks for sharing information has been highlighted in the 2010 report of the Organisation for Economic Co-Operation and Development (OECD) *(14)*. This report, which focuses on the challenges facing the world's most advanced countries in improving health care efficiency (but also encompasses emerging countries like Chile, Mexico, and Turkey), stresses the need for new legal frameworks which allow for sharing of health related information between health-care professions within and across health care organizations, as well as across organizational and geographical boundaries. The report notes that very few countries in its remit have really addressed these challenges: "…[G]eneralised uncertainty on how existing legal frameworks apply to health ICT systems, privacy concerns constitute one of the most difficult barriers to overcome if widespread implementation of ICTs is to be achieved" *(14)*.

Concerns with privacy in eHealth are not, however, the preserve of the high-income countries. A recent study titled eHealth Privacy in Developing Countries funded by the International Development Research Centre (IDRC) and conducted by researchers at the London School of Economics *(15)*, argued that the processing of information ranging from simple communication between patients and medical staff to complex sharing of data between care institutions is integral to good health care. The results of the project made clear however that many developing nations are poorly equipped to maintain adequate levels of patient privacy that such processing of health information demands:

---

1   See also the United Nations *World population prospects* (2010 revision).

> *In developing countries and humanitarian relief operations, where people are most vulnerable, worryingly there is little consideration of privacy policy and technology. In fact, where poor privacy practices may make already vulnerable people even more vulnerable, privacy is often perceived as an impediment to their care. Where it matters most is where it is mostly ignored (15).*

Many challenges for fostering a respect for patient privacy in developing nations may exist because of financial constraints, which make it hard to use more sophisticated health information security tools or to invest significantly in training health-care professionals on how to uphold ethical principles of privacy. To take an example from India, it may be argued that financial constraints are not the most significant limiting factor. Dr Aabha Nagral, writing in the Indian Journal of Medical Ethics in 1995, notes that "the same doctor, who, while dealing with patients in public hospitals, seems never to have cultivated any respect for their privacy, changes his attitude when dealing with patients in a private hospital. The sad truth is that a poor patient is taken for granted" *(16)*.

A 2009 study *(17)* on hospital doctors' understanding of ethics, including respect for patient privacy, revealed that there was a lack of proper and detailed knowledge of such duties among doctors. Shailaja Tetali *(18)* commenting in the same journal states:

> *as medical professionals, we generally do not give much thought to patients' feelings, especially with regard to their personal privacy. What could be the reasons for this apparent lack of sensitivity? Medical students in India are not formally taught about doctor-patient interactions. Ignorance among both doctors and patients about patient rights, and the asymmetry of information between them has ensured that patients do not have a voice of their own.*

The IDRC report states it is vital that proper systems of privacy protection in health care are initiated in developing countries. The authors argue that in countries where poor privacy protection is in place, patients are often unwilling to seek treatment for conditions where stigma and social exclusion will follow if a diagnosis is publically known. Thus if patients with conditions such as HIV/AIDS are to be properly supported, they must be willing to come forward, which in turn means that health care systems must ensure that the necessary procedures are in place to maintain the trust that patients have placed in them.

Ideally such systems would be based in legal frameworks which are well understood and enforced. The IDRC report notes, however, that in countries where such legislation is lacking, health-care providers have resorted to practical solutions to try to meet their patients' need for privacy. An example is given of an HIV support service in South Africa where SMS messages giving patients important information about their diagnosis or treatment are disguised as messages from friends about sports results. In this way the patient is protected should their SMS messages be read by another family member. As explored extensively in another volume in this series, eHealth also has uses in countries with more patient focused privacy legislation. An example would be the successful eHealth project in Mexico, Vidanet (19), which supports HIV/AIDS patients with text messages reminding them to take their anti-HIV drugs, keep their doctors' appointments, and stay up to date on their lab tests. The IDRC report notes however that the Vidanet service may become less popular as a result of new Mexican legislation which enforces the registration of all SIM cards. While such legislation may be a sound response to fighting corruption and gang activity, it is unfortunate that it might at the same time compromise public health, and provides a very good case for better and wider ranging health impact assessment for all legislation.

This evidence from important bodies such as OECD and IDRC makes clear therefore that appropriate legislation and systems to protect patient privacy are core elements of ensuring a good level of eHealth use. Accordingly the second global survey on eHealth sought to gain a better understanding of the extent to which targeted eHealth privacy issues had been considered in existing legislation. The results discussed below will highlight that there is still progress to be made in this matter, across both developed and less developed regions of the world.

1.3 Privacy or confidentiality of EHRs - a note on terminology

The terms privacy and confidentiality are sometimes distinguished on the basis that privacy refers to physical matters, while confidentiality refers to informational material *(20)*. According to that construction if a stranger walks into a consulting room and sees a patient being examined by a doctor the patient's privacy is violated, whereas if the same stranger later picks up the patient's health record, confidentiality is violated.

While this distinction is useful to some extent, it does not help in the discussion of the two concepts as they apply to EHRs, which are of course necessarily records of information. In this report the terms privacy and confidentiality are distinguished with reference to the relationship between the parties concerned by a piece of information. Privacy of information is construed as a general concept which reflects both the individual and public interest in the ability to keep information away from public view. Confidentiality, on the other hand, has to do with relationships and the rules that govern how information is shared within them. A piece of information which the subject of the information considers private will be shared within relationships which he or she considers confidential and where agreed rules of confidentiality apply. Such rules may be formalized in laws or codes of conduct, but they may also be based on cultural norms.

In this report the focus is primarily on the principle of privacy of health related information, that is the generic interest a patient has in being able to control who has access to his or her information. The practical rules of confidentiality that provide for how privacy is to be respected in the doctor-patient relationship are not discussed in detail.

2 The ethical and legal aspects of privacy in health care: a literature review

The present report explores the extent to which the respondent countries have a legal system in place for the protection of privacy in eHealth. In order to better understand and contextualize the answers to the survey discussed below, it will be useful to review the general literature on ethical and legal aspects of privacy in health care.

In order to provide as comprehensive a view as possible on the way in which the concept of privacy is understood in eHealth, context searches were conducted of PubMed, Social Sciences Review Network and Google Scholar using the terms 'legal', 'ethics', 'privacy', 'confidentiality', 'human rights', 'governance', 'consent', 'patient rights', and 'regulation' in conjunction with the term 'electronic health records'. Over 200 articles published in the period 2005 to 2010 were accessed, and many additional references within articles consulted. The literature review which follows does not however offer an exhaustive overview of all references. Many were too specialized on specific privacy needs of certain areas of health care, such as mental or sexual health privacy, to be relevant to a high level overview; others were very focused on technical means of achieving privacy, such as de-identification, rather than on the principle itself. The review does however draw on the literature which deals with the wider ethical and legal issues of privacy in health care. It is divided into five parts: ethical concepts; legal background; binding international law; international guidelines; and national law.

2.1 Privacy of health related information as an ethical concept

It is well accepted that the practice of health care is extremely information intensive *(21)* – clinical treatment, as well as coverage and payment, depend profoundly on robust, accurate, appropriate, and timely information – and that information is a vital component of modern health care systems *(22)*. The taking of a patient's history has been a core element of the health care encounter since medical practice began, and some form of record keeping of encounters between the clinician and patient has been central to providing care, even if in ancient times the clinician relied solely on his memory to record such information. Record keeping remains a core tenet of health care, although the advent of advanced testing, genetic profiling, and the techniques of medical imaging have hugely increased the volume and detail of health information in the past decades. The fully integrated, accessible, secure, and searchable EHR is both a vehicle for much needed change in health care organization – indeed many would say it is the Holy Grail of eHealth *(23, 24)* – but it also poses a significant potential threat to privacy in health care, and as a result it is important to develop specific ethical and legal frameworks for the protection of privacy in such records.

For most health-care professionals the requirement that health related information should be kept private, is a core element of ensuring that the trust the patient places in the clinician by sharing sensitive information is not violated. A common reference point for the ethical value of trust in the privacy of the doctor-patient relationship is the ancient Hippocratic Oath, which has for more than two thousand years been central to definitions of the ethical practice of health care. The Oath, which in its ancient form is only about 350 words long, declares on the matter of privacy:

> *What I may see or hear in the course of the treatment or even outside of the treatment in regard to the life of men, which on no account must be spread abroad, I will keep to myself, holding such things shameful to be spoken about (25).*

Although there are different interpretations of the meaning of this part of the Oath, with some scholars claiming that historically this was not concerned with privacy but more with a duty not to dishonour the patient by speaking badly of him or her *(26)*, it is commonly accepted that it is the basis of good ethical practice in handling patient information and encapsulates the duty of a doctor to maintain the privacy of his or her patient *(27)*.

The core ideas of the Oath have been translated into a wide range of modern declarations which, while maintaining the concept of respect for privacy, have added concessions to the need to protect individuals and facilitate the work of fellow physicians. The 1980 Principles of Medical Ethics of the American Medical Association thus states "A physician shall respect the rights of patients, colleagues, and other health professionals, and shall safeguard patient confidences and privacy within the constraints of the law" *(28)*.

While the United States of America's southern neighbour Chile was even more specific in its 2008 Code of Medical Ethics, which provides in Article 31 that physicians must respect the confidentiality of any information regarding their patients, whether it has been obtained through verbal exchange with them or through laboratory exams and surgical procedures; but also foresees it as legitimate to breach confidentiality in some cases that include illnesses that must legally be declared to the authorities (e.g. syphilis), and disclosures necessary to avoid severe harm to the patient or to other persons *(29)*.

The change in construction of medical privacy noted in these two examples does not invalidate the importance of the Hippocratic Oath and the ethical concept of privacy, but rather underlines the complexity of privacy and the range of competing ethical concepts that it has to support. Beauchamp and Childress, in their textbook *Principles of biomedical ethics (30)* which has for many years been the touchstone of understanding medical ethics around the world, famously reduce all medical ethics into four core principles:

- Respect for autonomy. Health-care professionals and health care systems should respect the decision-making capacities of autonomous persons and enable individuals to make reasoned and informed choices.

- Beneficence. Health-care professionals and health care systems should act in a way that benefits the patient, which will require a careful balancing of benefits of treatment against the risks and costs.

- Non-maleficence. Health-care professionals and health care systems should not harm the patient; while accepting that avoiding any treatment may involve some form of harm, such harm should not be disproportionate to the benefits of treatment.

- Justice. Health-care professionals and health care systems should distribute the benefits, risks, and costs of health care fairly, so that patients in similar positions may be treated in a similar manner.

If these principles are accepted as valid then it is worth considering briefly the way they are applied to a respect for privacy in EHRs.

A respect for health information privacy based in autonomy is perhaps the easiest to understand and the most closely related to common human rights concepts. The concept of autonomy is based fundamentally on the right of every competent adult to make decisions for him or herself. In the practice of the protection of privacy in health law, the autonomy of the patient is usually upheld by reference to concepts of consent. Thus most legislation on health records includes the requirement to seek a patient's consent before collecting, processing, or sharing health related information.

The respect for autonomy is however often tempered by consequentialist arguments of beneficence and non-maleficence. Thus most legislations, as noted in the reference to the American and Chilean codes of medical ethics above, include provisions which override a duty to respect privacy when a third party should be protected from risk of a contagious disease, or when the safety of the patient is at risk unless specialist care can be obtained. It should be noted that among scholars of medical ethics there is a considerable body of opinion which supports a duty of privacy tempered by an ability of the physician to decide that it is in the patient's or public interest to override that duty on the basis of foreseeable consequences if a third party is not warned of a risk. A new range of arguments is now also beginning to develop on the need to temper an absolute duty of privacy with a public duty to the advancement of medicine (31).

The argument on the consequential value of privacy (32) is closely tied to Beauchamp and Childress' idea of fidelity as a reason for maintaining the duty of privacy. Here the argument is that it is important to the ongoing faith of the patient in the doctor-patient relationship that implicit and explicit promises of privacy are kept. Beauchamp and Childress argue that "the context of medical practice requires disclosure of private information, and therefore a failure of fidelity tears at a significant dimension of the doctor–patient relationship" (32).

The ethical foundation of the respect for privacy of medical records may therefore be seen as a bargain, between the health-care professional and the patient, but also a bargain between the values of respect for autonomy and the requirement that the physician should seek not to harm the patient and respect the trust placed in him or her. In ethical terms, a bargain between the relative values of autonomy, beneficence, non-maleficence, and justice. Rothstein (33) examines the validity of the bargain in the age of EHRs and argues that while the ethical basis of a respect for privacy is still strong, the changing nature of medical practice and the rise of eHealth tools such as EHRs, means that the way in which the bargain between doctor and patient is struck and maintained needs to be re-examined.

2.2 The protection of privacy of health related information through law

The role of law in health care is, among other things, to ensure that the ethical principles of autonomy, beneficence and justice are translated into practice, and to provide a framework in which any failure to implement the duties that arise from those ethical principles may be addressed – that is to create a realm of legal certainty in which health care may be practised. As well as these operational aspects, health care law also has a public health role, in which law is used to protect the people within its jurisdiction from disease (e.g. by making certain infectious diseases modifiable and limiting the right to social interaction of disease carriers in certain circumstances) and from accidents and adverse environmental impacts (e.g. through health and safety legislation including speed limits or food hygiene laws). Law also has a role in balancing the relationship between the care provider and recipient of care (through civil law, criminal law, the law of torts) as well as the equitable distribution of access to care (public and civil law) *(34)*.

The law on the protection of privacy, whether in health care or in any other aspect of human interaction, generally makes use of three devices: comprehensive laws, sectoral laws, and informal rules. Comprehensive laws, often based in human rights, outline the general concept of privacy and the relationships which give rise to a legal expectation that privacy will be maintained. Sectoral laws deal with the specific demands of privacy in a social interaction, which will include areas such as health care services, financial services, and legal services. In sectoral laws of privacy the focus is usually on creating a framework where the data subject, the patient or the client, is empowered to share information with a service provider so that the service provider can use that information in order to deliver services in a way best adapted to the patient's or client's needs. These first two legal tools are usually in the form of formal law which may be written legal statute, case law, or a mixture of both depending on the nature of the jurisdiction in which the laws are created. These formal laws may be complemented with low level legislation, informal rules, and self-regulation that help those with responsibilities under comprehensive or sectoral laws to translate their duties into action. This last area includes 'soft law' such as practice guidelines as well as social customs and norms of professions.

Many legal systems also use low level legislation, informal rules, and self-regulation to add greater granularity to sectoral laws on privacy. They are used to interpret the comprehensive or sectoral laws with reference to specific issues and settings in order to provide greater guidance and support to those who have to deliver on the requirements set out in comprehensive or sectoral laws. Some such rules may be crafted as guidelines for the implementation of laws (such as statutory instruments in English law), but they may also include codes of conduct of professional organizations or other guidelines for good practice. Such guidelines are common in the health care setting, where codes of professional ethics are often regarded by health-care professionals as equally important as any legal obligations, not least because a breach of the code of ethics could lead to disbarring from the profession, even in cases where direct legal sanction is not so harsh. In common law systems these rules will also be used in legal proceedings as a reference for norms of behaviour for a profession, against which the behaviour of a professional may be assessed.

Depending on their application, these three legal devices (comprehensive, sectoral or guidelines) can be complementary or entirely stand alone. Although a body of laws specifically dealing with privacy in EHRs is slowly developing in pockets around the world, it is argued by many in the field that the laws and regulations still lack sufficient granularity to really make them fit to balance the competing interests stemming from the use of EHRs *(35)*.

This volume is concerned with the laws through which legal systems construct the relationship between the doctor and patient, and in particular how the data which the former holds about the latter are treated. The survey examined the extent to which legal systems around the world have provided measures to safeguard the privacy of such data and the way in which such a duty is construed. The focus is therefore on comprehensive laws of privacy, as well as on sectoral laws governing the doctor-patient relationship. The laws and rules under discussion set the reasonable expectations and limits of the patient's right to privacy and establish how a doctor or other health-care professional collects, processes, stores, and uses his or her information concerning his or her health and health care.

A common source for the comprehensive and sectoral legislation on privacy that has been adopted by countries are the rights set out in international conventions and treaties. The next section provides an overview of the binding international legal instruments which address privacy, as well as non-binding international agreements which groups of countries have adopted and pledged to implement within their national legislation in some form. It should be noted that while a number of international laws and declarations that address privacy or privacy in health exist, no binding international legislation to date expressly addresses privacy in eHealth.

2.3 Binding international law on privacy of health related information

The Universal Declaration of Human Rights

The Universal Declaration of Human Rights was adopted in 1948 by the United Nations (UN) General Assembly in a direct response to the atrocities of the Second World War. It is an internationally binding law which seeks to protect core human rights to a common standard globally. The declaration consists of some thirty articles which cover all the core issues of human rights. Privacy is addressed in Article 12 which provides:

> *No one shall be subjected to arbitrary interference with his privacy, family, home or correspondence, nor to attacks upon his honour and reputation. Everyone has the right to the protection of the law against such interference or attacks.*

The International Court of Justice, which was established to settle disputes between nations on the application of the declaration, has not given any ruling which is specifically relevant to the interpretation of Article 12. The existence of Article 12 is however cited as the baseline of many disputes on privacy in national courts.

The European Convention on Human Rights

The Convention for the Protection of Human Rights and Fundamental Freedoms, which is commonly known as the European Convention on Human Rights, is a treaty established by the Council of Europe in 1950 and binding all members of the Council of Europe. Unlike the UN Declaration, an individual who believes that his or her rights under the convention have been breached may bring a case to the European Court of Human Rights. The judgments of the Court are binding on the states, which are obliged to execute them.

Article 8 of the convention creates a right to respect for private and family life:

> *1. Everyone has the right to respect for his private and family life, his home and his correspondence.*
>
> *2. There shall be no interference by a public authority with the exercise of this right except such as is in accordance with the law and is necessary in a democratic society in the interests of national security, public safety or the economic well-being of the country, for the prevention of disorder or crime, for the protection of health or morals, or for the protection of the rights and freedoms of others.*

The European Convention on Human Rights has been the starting point of much litigation, with Article 8 being no exception. It is clear however from even a simple reading of the Article that it is complex, since paragraph 1 sets out the precise rights which are to be guaranteed, but paragraph 2 provides for exceptions to that right. It immediately sets up the expectation that privacy, while being of central importance to human rights is not absolute and must sometimes be balanced against other public interests.

Case law has established that medical records fall with the rights of privacy in Article 8, with the case of *Z v. Finland* [1996] *(36)* being perhaps one of the clearest statements on this matter recently. In that case a medical advisor was ordered to disclose details from the applicant's medical file during the trial of her husband for manslaughter. According to the Court, it is a key principle that the confidentiality of health data is respected: "Any state measures compelling communication or disclosure of such information without the consent of the patient call for the most careful scrutiny" *(36)*.

The Court's conclusion in *Z v. Finland* [1996] was, however, that the disclosure of the witness's medical records was "necessary", within the meaning of Article 8 para. 2, for the purposes of a trial. The Court therefore established that the interests of a patient, and society as a whole, may be outweighed by the interest in investigation and prosecution of a crime. Mindful of the issues that this might raise, the Court went on to find that the publication of the witness's name and HIV status in the appeal court judgment was not justified, thus reminding national legislature that although the patient's right to privacy may be outweighed by other interests, waiver of privacy rights must be limited to a minimum.

In 2009 the European Court of Human Rights was called upon again to give guidance on balancing public and private interests in health record privacy. While in *Z v. Finland* [1996] the Court had made clear that in criminal proceedings on manslaughter the public interest required that patient records were made public, in *Colak and Tsakiridis v. Germany* [2010] *(37)*, it was asked to consider the balance in the competing interests of two individuals. In that case a patient with HIV expressly requested his doctor not to inform his partner about his HIV status. After his death his partner, who was by that time herself HIV positive, sought to sue the doctor for failing to protect her by informing her about her partners HIV status. It took three German Courts and the European Court of Human Rights to finally establish that the doctor was right to maintain his patient's confidentiality, even though in doing so his patient's partner was exposed to risk.

The case demonstrates that although competing interests often exist, the courts in countries which have adopted the European Convention on Human Rights give a very high position to the concept of patient autonomy, even if the exercise of such autonomy may put another at risk. Thus while consequentialist arguments have a place in understanding the way in which health record privacy is to be interpreted, such interpretation will not always swing in favour of avoidance of harm to a third party. On a theoretical level this is made clear in Kottow's arguments when he pleads for an absolutist construction of the duty of privacy arguing that any dilution of the duty to respect the privacy of the patient is a significant threat to the integrity of the doctor-patient relationship *(32)*.

European Union Directive on the protection of individuals with regard to the processing of personal data and on the free movement of such data

In the European Union (EU) health care is regulated at national, not federal, EU level. At federal level, Article 168 of the Treaty on the Functioning of the European Union sets the requirement that a high level of human health protection is to be ensured in the definition and implementation of all EU policies and activities. However, the treaty also requires that decisions relating to the provision of health care services are taken at the national or local level (the legal principle of subsidiarity). The EU thus has only a limited legal competency on health matters, which can be used to adopt measures that complement national initiatives, or to adopt incentive measures designed to protect and improve human health, in particular to combat the major cross-border health scourges. The European Data Protection Directive is the EU level legislation on privacy to which all Member States in the EU must conform. It sets basic rights of privacy, but the exact interpretation of the practical exercise of those rights are decided in national legislation, which implements the Directive. Thus a certain level of legal certainty around health related privacy exists at EU level, but substantial variations still remain in the fine detail of the implementation of those rights in the Member States.

In Article 8 of the Directive a special status is accorded to all medical and health related information and prohibits the processing of health related data unless one of four exceptions is met:

- Explicit informed consent has been obtained from the data subject (Article 8(2)(a)); or
- Data processing is in the vital interests of the patient or of another person who is physically or legally incapable of giving consent (Article 8(2)(c)); or
- The processing of health data is required for the purposes of preventive medicine, medical diagnosis, the provision of care or treatment, or the management of health-care services AND the personal data in question are processed by a health professional (Article 8(3)); or
- There is a substantial public interest in the processing (Article 8(4)).

In order to help Member States interpret their duties under the Directive a data protection working party composed of the representatives of the national data protection authorities has been established. Its function is to advise the European Commission on the implementation of the Directive in the Member States. It is known as the Article 29 Data Protection Working Party and is referred to as the DPWP in this document. The working papers of the DPWP have no binding legal authority, but because they represent the common understanding of the data protection authorities of the Member States they may be used as evidence of common best practice in any litigation.

In 2007 the DPWP gave guidance on the processing of personal data in EHRs in one of its working papers *(38)*. The DPWP considered in some detail the extent to which each of the four possible exemptions under Article 8 of the Directive (as listed above) could be applied in the context of an EHR: consent, vital interests, care provision, and public interest. The DPWP's deliberations on the role of privacy in EHRs is discussed below in order to provide an example of some of the issues which legal policy-makers consider when seeking to balance the competing interests in privacy of EHRs.

Consent: The DPWP did not see consent as a valid basis for processing data in an EHR. The guidance argued that because the creation of a medical record is a necessary and unavoidable consequence of care provision, a health professional may be required to process personal data in an EHR, and thus withholding of consent may be to the patient's detriment. If withholding consent could be to a patient's detriment, then such consent would not be freely given as required in Article 8(2)(a).

Vital interest: The DPWP argued that in the medical context a 'vital interest' would have to be for life-saving treatment in a context where the patient is not able to express him- or herself. Accordingly they argued that this exception could not be used for routine processing of health information in an EHR.

Health care provision: The full text of Article 8(3) requires that the personal data in question are "required" for provision of care and the personal data are processed by a health professional subject "under national law or rules established by national competent bodies to the obligation of professional secrecy or by another person also subject to an equivalent obligation of secrecy"(41). The DPWP argued strongly against the use of this exemption to legitimate the creation of an EHR, principally because it sees an EHR as giving access to medical histories to health-care professionals who were not party to the previous treatment documented in the EHR and therefore could not have been considered by the patient when entering into the trusted relationship with the primary carer. Thus the most common justification of an EHR system – that it improves the provision of health care – is not seen as sufficient by the DPWP to legitimate the collection of medical data in such a system.

Substantial public interest: The DPWP notes that since consent, vital interests, and medical care (Article 8(2)(a) and (3)), would probably not be sufficient to allow an EHR to be established, Member States should consider the possibility of adopting special regulations to safeguard privacy in EHR on the basis that an EHR is in itself a matter of public interest. Such legal provision would have to provide specific and suitable safeguards for the protection of privacy with an EHR system and would have to be duly notified with the European Commission.

The DPWP went on to consider what a legal framework for data protection in an EHR system as provided for under Article 8(4) might look like. The DPWP noted that if the safeguards for data privacy in an EHR are well drafted, it may be legitimate to offer an opt-out system. They argued that such an opt-out system would assume that for general health information a patient has opted-in to the system unless he or she explicitly opts-out. The DPWP suggested however that given that an EHR will contain many different types of information such an opt-in/ opt-out system should be incremental – thus a general opt-out might apply, but a specific opt-in would be necessary for processing especially sensitive information such as information about mental health or sexually transmitted infections. The DPWP also suggested that rules should provide that a patient can prevent a particular category of medical professional seeing a particular category of his or her data. It did not say whether such suppression of data should be visible on the face of the record, but notes the value of the use of the 'sealed envelope' technique.

The DPWP also argued that the rules concerning an EHR should allow only those health-care professionals or authorized personnel of health care institutions who are presently involved in the patient's treatment to have access, and that there must be a relationship of actual and current treatment between the patient and the health-care professional wanting access to his or her EHR. They suggested that this could be well supported by modular access rights, forming categories of medical data in an EHR system to which access is limited to specific categories of health-care professionals or institutions. Thus the EHR could contain an emergency data set with relatively low access controls while highly sensitive data could be accessible only by the treating primary care physician. The DPWP recognized that patients should have access to the data held in the EHR, thus the rules for an EHR system must address issues of patient access and should consider granting access to patients so that they can add to the record themselves.

The UN Declaration on Human Rights, European Convention on Human Rights, and the European Data Protection Directive are the main binding legal instruments at international level which address privacy and which can be applied to EHRs. It is noteworthy that two of the three international legal texts are addressed to Europe only. The effect of this fact is seen in the eHealth survey in which the European Region consistently reports a more developed legal protection of health related data than other regions. However, based on the wide cultural acceptance of the concept of privacy (as discussed above) it was nevertheless deemed useful to begin the survey on legal protection of privacy in EHR data by asking respondents to clarify if their countries have adopted legislation which would give patients the rights to privacy along the lines set out in these international legal instruments. The survey begins by looking at the existence of a protection of privacy law as set out in the UN declaration and the European convention, and asks respondents to identify any legislation that would address the rights contained in the guidance of the DPWP, such as patients' rights to access and control.

2.4 International non-binding agreements

Convention for the Protection of Individuals with regard to Automatic Processing of Personal Data

The 1981 Convention (also called Convention 108), which is based on Article 8 of the European Convention on Human Rights, sets out to ensure every individual, regardless of nationality or residence, can secure his or her privacy in the processing of personal data. The legislation was the first in the world to address the special privacy issues raised by automatic processing, but is now rather dated as computing power has increased exponentially since it was drafted.

Under Convention 108, the parties are required to take the necessary steps in their domestic legislation to apply the principles it lays down in order to ensure respect in their territory for the fundamental human rights of all individuals with regard to processing of personal data. The principles are particularly concerned with data quality, namely:

- data must be obtained and automatically processed fairly and lawfully;
- data must be recorded for specified and legitimate purposes;
- data must not be used in a way incompatible with those purposes;
- data must be stored only for as long as is required for these purposes;
- data must be recorded in an adequate, relevant, and non-excessive proportional) manner vis-à-vis the said purposes; and
- data must be accurate.

Convention 108 also establishes everyone's right to have access to the data concerning them and to obtain rectification or deletion of these data if they have been processed unlawfully. With respect to medical data, or data concerning the health of the data subject the convention expressly prohibits such processing unless it is provided for in national law and such law provides appropriate safeguards. As a result it is unlawful to process medical information about a person unless one has a legal basis to do so, such as an existing doctor-patient relationship.

Council of Europe Recommendation No. R (97) 5 on the protection of medical data

Recommendation No. R (97) 5 was adopted by the Council of Minister of the Council of Europe, in 1997 to replace Recommendation No. R (81) 1 on regulations for automated medical data banks. It was deemed to be necessary because of the extensive computerization of the entire health sector (doctors, hospital and public health management, research, pharmacists) and of sectors other than health (employment, insurance), together with the progress made in medical science, especially genetics, all of which were seen to pose new problems for the protection of medical data. It provides that legislation protecting privacy should apply to all medical data, whether processed by a doctor or by another person.

WHO: A Declaration on the Promotion of Patients' Rights in Europe

The role of international codes on medical ethics has already been noted above, but it is worth noting that in 1994 WHO has also adopted a declaration through which it encouraged all its Member States to adopt legislation or regulations which specify the rights, entitlements, and responsibilities of patients, health professionals, and health care institutions with respect to medical data privacy. It is a matter for decision by countries as to how they might make use of a document such as this when reviewing their present policies and legislative support to patients' rights.

Generally the declaration notes: "1.2 Everyone has the right to self-determination. 1.4 Everyone has the right to respect for his or her privacy". And on matters of privacy WHO declares in Article 4:

> *4.1 All information about a patient's health status, medical condition, diagnosis, prognosis and treatment and all other information of a personal kind must be kept confidential, even after death.*
>
> *4.2 Confidential information can only be disclosed if the patient gives explicit consent or if the law expressly provides for this. Consent may be presumed where disclosure is to other health care providers involved in that patient's treatment.*
>
> *4.3 All identifiable patient data must be protected. The protection of the data must be appropriate to the manner of their storage. Human substances from which identifiable data can be derived must be likewise protected.*
>
> *4.4 Patients have the right of access to their medical files and technical records and to any other files and records pertaining to their diagnosis, treatment and care and to receive a copy of their own files and records or parts thereof. Such access excludes data concerning third parties.*
>
> *4.5 Patients have the right to require the correction, completion, deletion, clarification and/or updating of personal and medical data concerning them which are inaccurate, incomplete, ambiguous or outdated, or which are not relevant to the purposes of diagnosis, treatment and care.*
>
> *4.6 There can be no intrusion into a patient's private and family life unless and only if, in addition to the patient consenting to it, it can be justified as necessary to the patient's diagnosis, treatment and care.*
>
> *4.7 Medical interventions may only be carried out when there is proper respect shown for the privacy of the individual. This means that a given intervention may be carried out only in the presence of those persons who are necessary for the intervention unless the patient consents or requests otherwise.*
>
> *4.8 Patients admitted to health care establishments have the right to expect physical facilities which ensure privacy, particularly when health care providers are offering them personal care or carrying out examinations and treatment.*

In terms of international law it is clear then that binding high-level laws on a right to privacy exist, and that in some cases these have been used extensively to address issues of privacy with respect to health related data. Of these, the European Convention on Human Rights is perhaps the strongest, having delivered clear guidelines to Member States on balancing the rights of individual patients and the public at large. The decisions in *Z v. Finland* [1996] and *Colak and Tsakiridis v. Germany* [2010] make especially clear that rights to privacy are not absolute and must be balanced against identifiable risk to a third party as well as risk to the integrity of the doctor-patient relationship and the trust that patients place in that relationship.

To date however neither binding nor non-binding legislation has been adopted specifically on EHRs; the nearest specific treatment is the guidance of the Data Protection Working Party on the application of the EU Data Protection Directive to EHRs. Some countries have however adopted legislation at national level to address the special privacy needs raised by EHRs. This is discussed in general in the next section and then exemplified by reference to the applicable national level legislation in Brazil and the USA.

2.5 National law on privacy of health related information

Privacy International, in their 2006 survey of privacy and human rights laws *(39)*, demonstrate that most countries around the world have some form of privacy protection in law which govern the collection, use, and dissemination of personal information by both the public and private sectors.

Their survey makes clear however that while comprehensive human rights laws, such as constitutions or civil rights laws, often address some element of informational privacy, only a few countries have specific sectoral legislation addressing medical privacy; even fewer have legislation which specifically covers privacy and other patients' rights in EHRs. The eHealth survey found equally that although a reasonably high level of comprehensive laws addressing certain aspects of privacy that apply to EHRs existed, only a few countries have laws which specifically address the issue of medical records privacy, and even fewer have laws focused on privacy of EHRs.

The work of Sarabdeen and Ishak *(40)* provides a typical example of a range of laws applying to the privacy which exist in many countries. From their list it may be noted that while Malaysia has a good range of general privacy laws (as well as some specific privacy laws in banking and business) rights to privacy in health care have to be extrapolated from the general laws, as follows.

- Penal Code
- Computer Crimes Act 1997
- Digital Signature Act 1997
- Communication and Multimedia Act 1998
- Official Secrets Act 1972
- National Land Code 1965
- Consumer Protection Act 1999
- Banking and the Financial Institutions Act 1989

Based on their assessment of these laws Sarabdeen and Ishak conclude that although a basic level of privacy protection is provided for, the fact that no specific medical record privacy legislation exists means only minimal regulations exist. This, they argue, has a considerable negative impact on the potential use of ICT in health care as it means that law "may not be able to strike a balance between the private interest of information privacy and the government's interest to collect, use and store the information" *(40)*.

In order to understand more fully the potential impact of comprehensive privacy legislation and sectoral EHR privacy legislation, Boxes 1 and 2 show the way in which two countries have responded to the requirement to protect the privacy of health related information, while at the same time allowing such information to be shared in order to provide care to the individual or promote public health. Brazil has been chosen as an example of a country with a range of generic privacy laws coupled with soft law regulation on the health care field (Box 1), while the USA has been chosen as an example of a country with a high level of specific eHealth privacy legislation (Box 2).

Box 1. Health care privacy: generic and soft laws in Brazil

Constitutional rights to privacy

The Federal Constitution of Brazil asserts the inviolable right to privacy and private life. The confidentiality of all correspondence and data is upheld, except when required by court order for the purposes of criminal investigation. The Penal Code stipulates detention of up to one year, and/or indemnity payments for all violations of privacy law. The Civil Code reinforces the right to privacy and the role of the judiciary as a protector of this right.

In addition, the law of Habeas Data (a constitutional writ granted by the Brazilian State) ensures the ability of individuals to access their personal data as held by any public entity. It also guarantees the right to update and correct any information or data relating to them.

Information Technology National Policy

Regulated by federal law, the Information Technology National Policy aims to establish legal and technical mechanisms and instruments to protect informational rights. This includes the secrecy of data, constitutional privacy rights, and the right to free access and correction of personal information held in public and private databases. It also institutes quality standards for information technology products and services by means of registration and certification. For private institutions, access to and rectification of personal data are assured by the Consumer Protection Code.

Federal Council of Medicine

Medical data management is regulated by the Federal Council of Medicine (FCM). As of 2007, the council authorizes the digitalization of medical records provided those records meet certain quality standards. The FCM provides a manual that outlines these requirements (Manual de Certificação para Sistemas de Registro Eletrônico em Saúde [Manual for the Certification of Electronic Health Records]). The council also demands the creation of specialized systems that would manage digital medical information in accordance with the manual.

Privacy law and electronic health records

Brazil has not adopted specific EHR privacy legislation. However a reasonably high level of technical privacy protection requirements are enforced by Brazilian Federal Law, which demands that any legally valid electronic document must be certified by the Comitê Gestor Infra-estrutura de Chaves Públicas, the organization operating the official Brazilian public infrastructure to ensure the authenticity, integrity, and security of information. In addition to these technical measures, the FCM has established six of its own certification systems. The council has also stated the need for respecting quality standards, and promotes the creation of specific systems designed to manage electronic information in accordance with their manual of digital certification.

Box 2. Health care privacy: specific eHealth laws in the USA

Constitutional and common law rights to privacy
There is no constitutional right to privacy in the United States, but tort law-based rights to protection against the invasion of privacy as stated in the Prosser's Restatement (Second) of Torts at §§ 652A-652 includes the right to privacy of communications (which includes medical records).

Health information privacy
The Office for Civil Rights enforces the Health Insurance Portability and Accountability Act (HIPAA) and the HIPAA Privacy Rule, which protect the privacy of individually identifiable health information.

Health data processing
HIPAA addresses the way in which privacy in health related information is to be ensured by health-care professionals and the administrative bodies concerned with the organization and reimbursement of health care. HIPAA is not exclusively about EHRs, but covers any person identifiable piece of health information which a covered entity collects from an individual or receives from another entity relating (inter alia) to past, present, or future physical or mental health conditions. HIPAA rules apply to written, image, and oral data regardless of the medium on which they are stored.

HIPPA and privacy
The HIPAA Privacy Rule establishes national standards to protect individuals' medical records and other personal health information and applies to health plans, health care clearinghouses, and those health-care providers that conduct certain health care transactions electronically. The rule requires appropriate safeguards to protect the privacy of personal health information, and sets limits and conditions on the uses and disclosures that may be made of such information without patient authorization. The rule also gives patients rights over their health information, including rights to examine and obtain a copy of their health records, and to request corrections.

HIPAA and data sharing
Within the context of the American Recovery and Reinvention Act (ARRA) of 2009 the USA adopted legislation to promote the use of EHRs in the Health Information Technology for Economic and Clinical Health (HITECH) Act, which creates significant incentives for an expanded use of electronic health records. In seeking to better protect the privacy of patients the HITECH Act requires HIPAA-covered entities to provide notification to affected individuals and to the Secretary of the Department of Health and Human Services (HSS) following the discovery of a breach of unsecured protected health information. In addition, in some cases, HITECH requires covered entities to provide notification to the media of breaches. In the case of a breach of unsecured protected health information at or by a business associate of a covered entity, the act requires the business associate to notify the covered entity of the breach. It also requires the HHS to post on its web site a list of covered entities that experience breaches of unsecured protected health information involving more than 500 individuals.

Use of EHRs in Brazil

At present electronic records and messages in health care are used in health care in Brazil primarily for administrative purposes such as insurance reimbursement, patient registration, and appointment making. The use of comprehensive electronic health records is still limited to only a select number of hospitals and health organizations around the country (41). However, in 2012, a nationwide electronic health record system will be implemented in all public health institutions. This project is expected to be completed in 2014 and will contain the records of about 200 million people. Brazil's legislative response to privacy in EHRs is a reasonably representative example of the most common form of legal framework for personal privacy protection based in human rights laws found within a constitution, which is coupled with a few specific rights on privacy in telecommunications, and supported by a general medical ethical framework on a respect for privacy in the doctor-patient relationship. The law of Habeas Data, which was pioneered in Brazil and is now widely used in Latin America, gives a good level of protection to the individual, and allows for a good level of control over his or her data.

Brazil, like many other countries, has not however responded directly to the demands raised by the EHR, nor has it adapted the general medical legislation to the changing nature of the doctor-patient relationship. Although the concept of Habeas Data gives patients a baseline set of rights in terms of access and correction, there is no legislation which makes references to the wide range of technical solutions which may be used to make such rights applicable in EHRs, such as remote access, data tagging, and data obfuscation. It is interesting to note however that Brazil has responded quite extensively to the quality and security needs of using ICT in health care. This too is not unusual and while the adoption of technical tools such as public key infrastructure and certification are vital elements of ensuring that privacy can be maintained and monitored, it does not accord specific rights and duties to patients and health-care professionals – it is a technical response rather than a legal one.

Legislative responses to EHRs in the USA

The legislative response in the USA is an example of highly developed legal response focused on the potential threats and benefits of EHRs. It is implemented alongside technical infrastructure solutions to maintain privacy as well as a Security Rule which "...establishes national standards to protect individuals' electronic personal health information that is created, received, used, or maintained by a covered entity" (42).

Interestingly the USA, does not start from a fundamental rights perspective. In 2011 the US Supreme Court confirmed:

> "Like many other desirable things not included in the Constitution, "informational privacy" seems like a good idea — wherefore the People have enacted laws at the federal level and in the states restricting the government's collection and use of information. But it is up to the People to enact those laws, to shape them, and, when they think appropriate, to repeal them. A federal constitutional right to "informational privacy" does not exist" (43).

Yet a very detailed legislative framework has been developed to address the often competing needs of data sharing among health-care professionals and the individual rights of patients.

The most recent legislation in the HITECH Act is a particularly good example of this since it seeks to balance the need to have a clear public policy statement of respect for privacy in the doctor-patient relationship, while at the same time setting up a mechanism to allow the research community access to the wealth of data in longitudinal EHRs. HITECH recognizes the potential that EHRs pose for the wealth of a nation – the USA is remarkable in having been the first to address, through primary legislation (as opposed to use guidelines), the contribution EHRs can make to wealth as well as to health. The HITECH Act clarified pricing of the infrastructure services that are required to convert raw patient data into valuable data resources for research and public health, and it authorized data-holders to conduct commercial transactions when supplying data for public health and research. The opportunity for a similar response exists also in Europe where the Directive on Patients' Rights in Cross-Border Healthcare (44) has its legal roots in recognizing the market importance of cross-border care and the value of eHealth tools such as EHRs in facilitating the development of that market.

The analysis of the responses to the survey which follows will show the extent to which the two types of legal responses – comprehensive law rights in a general respect of privacy and specific sectoral legislation on EHR privacy – are sufficient in addressing the new legal and ethical issues made so clear by EHRs. While medical practice has for many centuries struggled with competing demands of individual rights and public health needs, the potential offered by EHRs makes this tension much more evident. The objective of the analysis of the survey responses to follow is therefore to establish if they are robust enough to provide a strong framework for regulating and balancing the competing interests in access and privacy which exist in EHRs. Furthermore, the responses will be reviewed to determine if, as Terry argues, the paradigm shift that EHRs create in the organization and delivery of health care (in which the patient data contained in longitudinal systems is comprehensive, portable, and manipulatable) opens such an immense potential for abuse that the old legislative responses are simply no longer fit for purpose (45).

It should be noted here that the eHealth survey did not ask questions about the vexed issue of medical record ownership. While the literature on ownership of health records is extensive, it is also divided and reflects many perspectives – including arguments that patient ownership of records would improve privacy and at the same time improve access to data for researchers *(46)*, and the opposed view that public rather than patient ownership of records would best support good health care service *(47)*. What emerges clearly from the literature is that the ownership of medical records is unclear. To some extent this has understandable roots in history: in simpler times medical records were generated and kept by general practitioners who looked after the patient for almost all their health care needs. The records were made on paper owned by the health-care professional and were seen as part of his or her business – indeed health care records are a key intangible asset in the sale of a general practice business and constitute the goodwill of the business.

However outside the sale of health care businesses, establishing the ownership of health care records will have little value in protecting the privacy of individuals whose information is contained in the record. For this discussion the key issue in EHRs is establishing what rights a patient may exercise over a record and how those rights are balanced with the rights of the clinician and the health care system. Accordingly the eHealth survey did not explore ownership, but instead explored the extent to which the patient had the right to access, correct, delete, or hide aspects of the EHR, and in how far the clinician had the right to share records with others for the purposes of treatment or research. The research discussed in this report thus reflects the sentiment expressed by Anderson who states simply:

> *Who owns the data held in electronic health information systems is a question of nominal importance that threatens to distract from more pressing work that needs to be done to protect privacy while realizing the public health benefits of interoperable health data networks (48).*

3 Analysis of survey results

 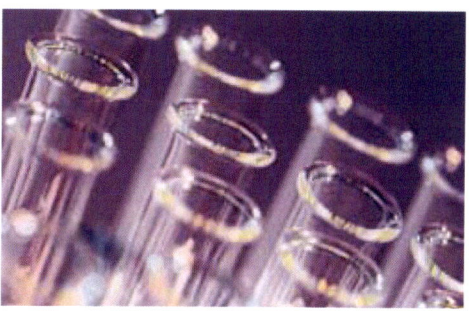 

The discussion of the literature above shows that respect for, and protection of, patient privacy has a well-established history in global legal systems. It is generally accepted that such protection of privacy is not only a fundamental right of the individual, but also a core requirement of how health care is practiced: respect for the privacy of the individual is crucial to the trust relationship between patient and health-care provider. The fact that this has been true for thousands of years is made plain by the fact that the Hippocratic Oath demanded privacy in 4th century BCE and is still the basis of the ethical duty of respect for privacy in the practice of health care today.

However, the more recent literature shows that scholars across disciplines – philosophy, sociology and medicine – have all noted that health care is changing. It is moving from being based in a long-term relationship between a patient a small number of doctors to a series of shorter relationships with a much wider range of health-care professionals, which may be conducted online or on the phone as well as through more traditional face-to-face interaction. In these changing circumstances it is becoming increasingly important not only to respect privacy in practice but also to demonstrate that breaches of the duty will not be tolerated. It is, in short, becoming more and more important to have a sound legal framework of privacy legislation directly applicable to health care as it is practiced today – whether that is in person or through an ICT medium.

3.1. General privacy legislation

The second global survey on eHealth asked a series of questions about the nature of the regulation of privacy in health care in order to ascertain if the regulatory environment was ready for a full and effective exploitation of eHealth solutions.

In order to establish a baseline on privacy protection, the first question of the survey addressing legal and ethical aspects of eHealth went back beyond any legislation to do with eHealth specifically and asked respondents if their country had enacted any form of legislation to protect the privacy of the individual based on concepts of privacy in human rights law. The first question on the legal and ethical aspects of eHealth in the survey sought to establish if privacy protection exists as a legal concept in the country:

> *Does your country have legislation to ensure privacy of personally identifiable data of individuals irrespective of whether it is in analog or digital format? If 'no' when do you expect your country to take this action?*

A footnote gives further clarification that, for the purposes of this question, 'personal identifiable data' is any information which can specifically identify an individual. This can include, but is not limited to, names, date of birth, addresses, telephone numbers, occupations, photographs, fingerprints – regardless of the format or medium in which it held. The responses to these, and indeed all the questions in the survey, were categorized both by WHO region and by World Bank income group. Details of these two groupings are set out in Appendix 1, along with the complete survey methodology.

Key trends

- A very significant proportion of all countries reported the existence of some level of privacy protection through legislation.
- The adoption of privacy legislation is higher in high- and middle-income countries than in lower-income countries.
- The European Region reports a higher level of privacy legislation adoption than the other regions of the world.
- Many countries that do not currently protect privacy through law are in the process of adopting such legislation and most foresee that it will be in place by 2015.

Results

A sizeable majority – almost 70% of the 113 responding countries – have some sort of privacy legislation in place (Figure 1). Figure 2 shows that the European Region has the highest uptake among WHO regions. A further analysis of the responses shows that in general higher-income countries have a higher prevalence of legal protection of privacy than lower-income countries (Figure 3).

Figure 1. Global levels of generic privacy legislation

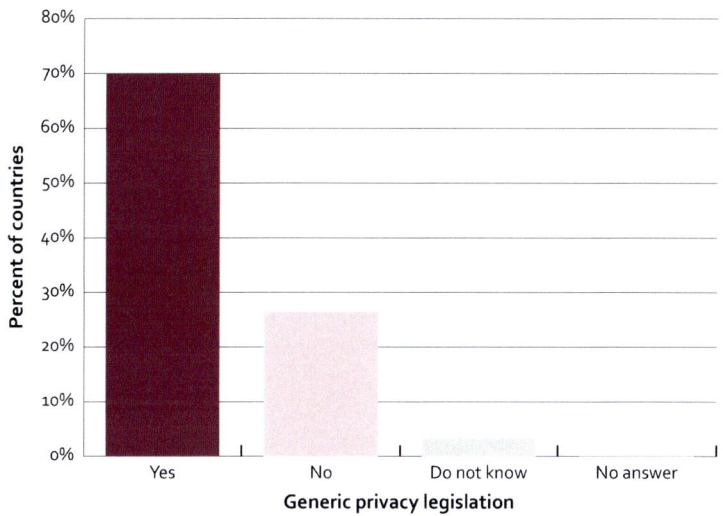

Figure 2. Countries with established generic privacy legislation, by WHO region

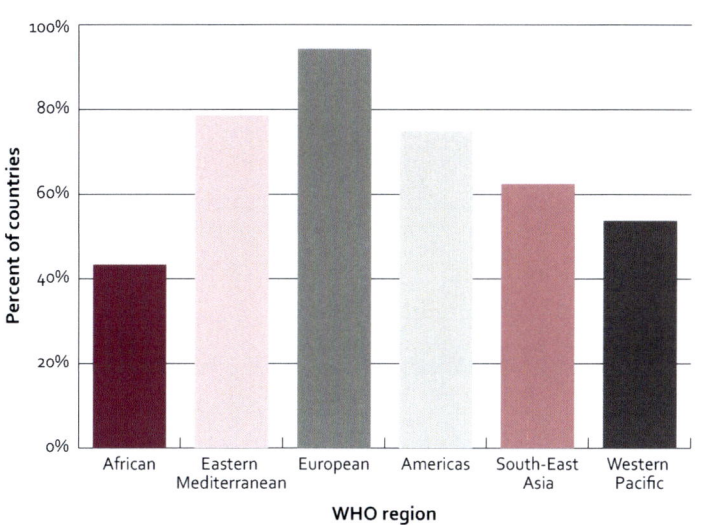

Figure 3. Countries with established generic privacy legislation, by World Bank income group

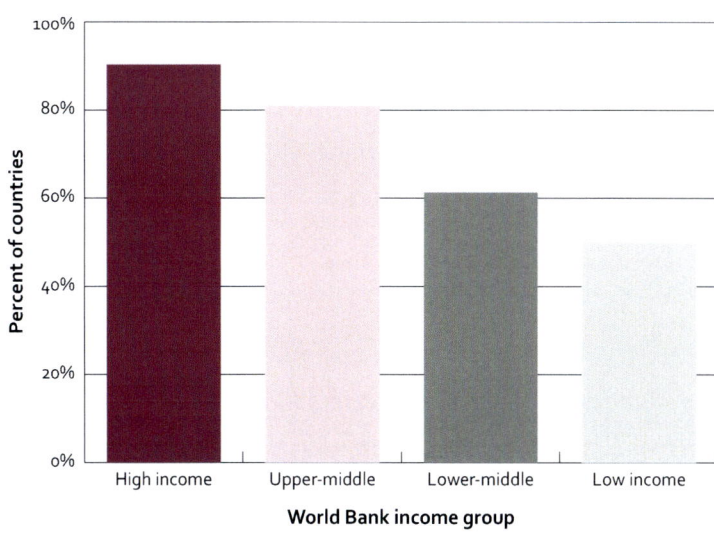

The general importance given to protection of privacy is evidenced also by the responses given in the linked question, in which those countries responding 'no' to the first question were asked to specify whether plans existed to enact privacy legislation in the near future. Of those answering that they had no general privacy legislation in place as yet, all showed that plans were under way to adopt such legislation in the coming years (Figure 4). If such targets are met, then 83% of the countries taking part in the survey will have some level of legal privacy protection in place by 2015.

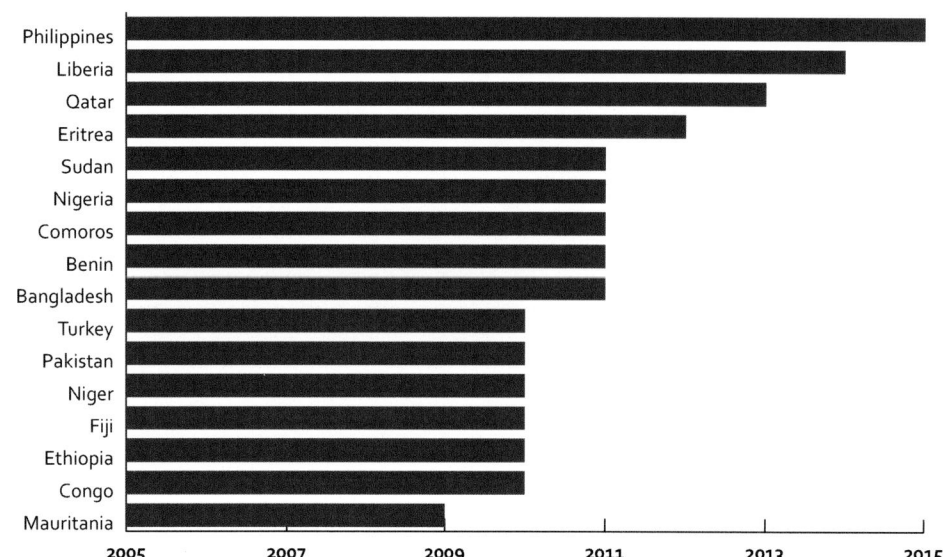

Figure 4. Year by which countries without generic privacy legislation intend to adopt privacy measures

Discussion

It is perhaps unsurprising that globally there is a reasonably high level of legal protection of privacy, not least because many global and supranational level legal texts demand of their signatories that privacy is protected. As noted in Section 2, the United Nations Declaration on Human Rights demands in Article 12 that "no one shall be subjected to arbitrary interference with his privacy, family, home or correspondence"; while Article 8 of the European Convention on Human Rights states that "Everyone has the right to respect for his private and family life, his home and his correspondence". In the EU the human rights based protection of privacy is taken one step further in requiring EU Member States to specifically regulate (and to protect) the processing of private data. The EU requires its Member States to enact legislation based on Directive 95/46/EC on the protection of individuals with regard to the processing of personal data and free movement of such data to "protect the fundamental rights and freedoms of natural persons, and in particular their right to privacy, with respect to the processing of personal data" (Article 1). The existence of this Directive will account for the fact that 94% of the countries in the European Region gave a positive response to the survey question.

However, while 70% of the global respondents reported that their country had privacy protecting legislation, some 27% of respondents reported that no privacy protecting legislation existed in their countries (the remaining 3% reported 'don't know'). It is important therefore to asses if the lack of such legislation is a significant impediment to the implementation of eHealth tools and solutions, since the objective of this survey as a whole was not to examine the extent to which fundamental human rights were protected around the world, but rather to establish how far eHealth is being used to support the health of citizens. The objective of the questions on legal protection of privacy was to establish if such protection existed – and perhaps to extrapolate from the existence of such legislation to the potential to exploit eHealth for the benefit of the citizens.

It is important here to ask if a country which does not have basic privacy legislation can nevertheless promote eHealth effectively. England could be a good case for exemplifying that privacy law per se is not needed to promote the use of eHealth tools and solutions. England, through its National Health Service Connecting for Health Programme, has made huge advances in driving the uptake of eHealth – encompassing nationally shared summary care records, electronic prescribing, a secure e-mail system for general practitioners, a facility for patients to choose and book appointments for secondary care, a comprehensive picture archiving system among many more elements.[2] Yet the law of England[3] does not include any specific legislation which protects the privacy of the individual. English law has neither a specific codification of privacy in a statute, nor an express reference to a legal right of privacy in its common law (case law); the Calcutt Committee of 1990 concluded that "nowhere have we found a wholly satisfactory statutory definition of privacy" (49). Historically therefore people seeking protection of their privacy (whether physical or informational) in England have had to rely on a piecemeal collection of related legislation on topics like harassment, breach of confidence, or data protection.

Despite the evident lack of privacy legislation per se, English citizens enjoy a high level of eHealth in their National Health Service. One might argue therefore that the absence of a fully fledged privacy law has not greatly hindered the English National Health Service in becoming one of the most advanced users of eHealth tools and solutions in the world. However, despite the experience of the National Health Service in England, many legal scholars (50) agree that a legal approach based upon the recognition of an explicit right to privacy would yield greater clarity, rigour, and coherence. Thus, although England enjoys a good level of medical data protection through common law and has a well-established system of information governance (51), it has been suggested that the lack of a simple right of privacy undermines general public confidence in the system (50).

It may be argued therefore that those countries which currently do not have a specific legal protection of privacy, may have greater difficulty in building the necessary confidence of their citizens in rolling out health programmes which are substantially underpinned by eHealth. A 2009 study (52) of patient opinions about the use of EHRs in the United States found that patients overwhelmingly recognized the potential for the electronic exchange of health information to improve the quality of health care and prevent medical errors, but that concerns about security and privacy held them back in fully embracing the potential of the EHR.

---

2   See http://www.connectingforhealth.nhs.uk
3   Note that the English legal system encompasses legislation in force in England and Wales; Scotland and Northern Ireland have a separate legal system.

3.2 EHR privacy legislation

In order to gain a greater understanding how the concept of privacy protection is interpreted with respect to health related information, the second set of questions within the GOe survey asked respondents if any legislation exists which is addressed specifically at protecting health related information held electronically in an EHR. This section of the survey therefore sought to establish whether countries have tried to address the complexity of privacy in health care, and in particular in eHealth-enabled health care, through legislation which provides guidelines on how the privacy of EHRs is to be assured.

Simple yes/no questions were asked on the existence of privacy legislation to safeguard health related information held electronically in an EHR. Health related data were defined as information recorded about an individual including their illnesses, and prescribed treatments, including details of prescribed medication, and any medical or surgical procedures undertaken as well as treatments received from other health-care providers.

Does your country have specific legislation to protect privacy of individuals' health-related data held in digitized format in an EMR or EHR? If no, when do you expect your country to take this action?

Key trends

- Globally only around one third of Member States have specific legislation to protect the privacy of information held in an EHR.
- Such legislation is much more common in high- and middle-income countries than in low-income countries.
- Special legislation is being planned in many countries, so that by 2012 almost two thirds of all countries responding to the survey should have such legislation on the statute book.

Results

To put the responses on legal protection of EHR data into context, it is important first to establish the prevalence of EHRs globally. Section 5 of the survey asked respondents to rate their use of different formats of patient information processing. The survey gave two options for information processing: paper or computerized and asked respondents to rate their use of the two formats as low (less than 25%); medium (more than 25% less than 50%; high (between 50 and 75%); and very high (more than 75%).

The results of the survey show that electronic processing of health information is now reasonably well-established at a global level – 44% of the responding countries recorded that they had a medium, high, or very high level of electronic processing of individual health information at a local level, although only 14% reported a high or very high level of electronic processing of health information (Figure 5).

Figure 5. Types of patient information in local health care facilities

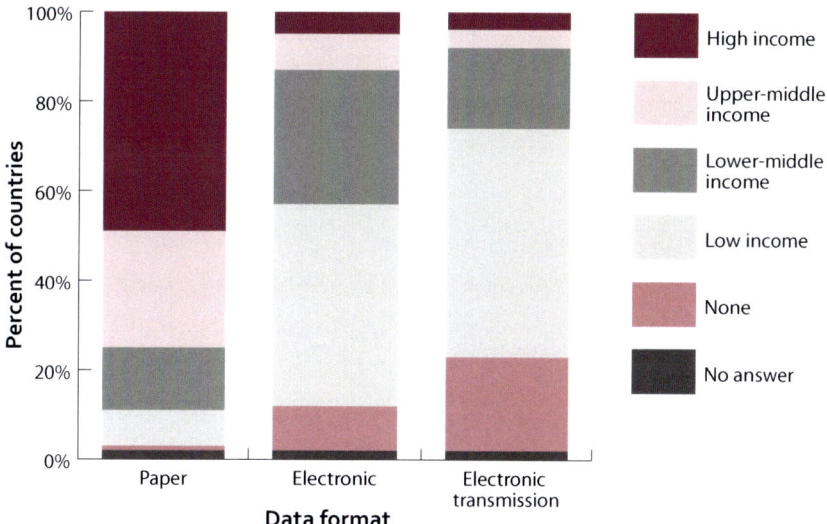

While not all electronic processing of health information will amount to the existence of an EHR, it is fair to say that a good proportion of the 44% responding positively will have some form of EHR. Setting the global responses for the question on the existence of legislation to protect data held in an EHR against that background, it can be seen that there is still room for progress, since only some 30% of the total 113 countries responding to the survey stated that they has such specific legislation (Figure 6).

Figure 6. Established legislation to protect privacy of digitized health-related data, globally

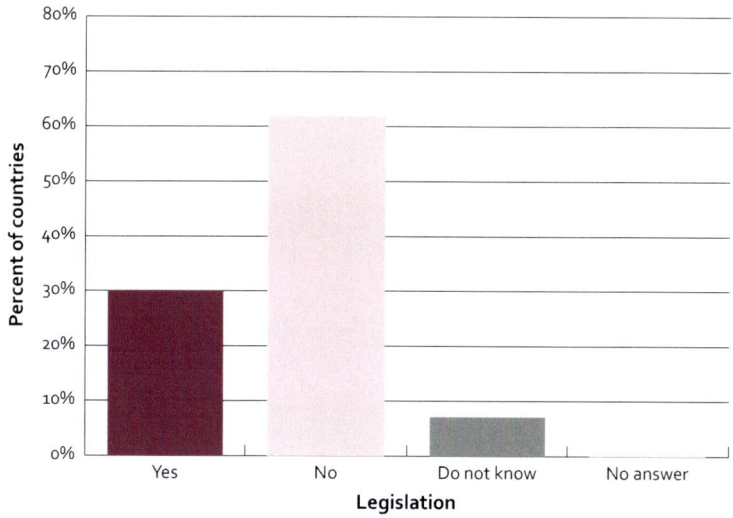

Although currently only approximately one third of responding countries provide such protection, it is worth noting that many reported having the implementation of such legislation on the agenda. Of the 70 countries that responded 'no' to the question above, 31 stated that by 2012 they would have such legislation in place. If these expectations are met, then by 2012 approximately 58% of the responding countries would have such legislation in place. The remaining 39 countries answering 'no' to the question showed no indication that such legislation would be enacted in the foreseeable future.

When the results were analysed by World Bank income group and WHO region (Figures 7 and 8), it was interesting to note that of the high-income countries, all those reporting the existence of such legislation are members of the EU or the European Economic Area. This may be attributed to the European Data Protection Directive which, while not requiring such specific legislation to be put in place, has provided a useful platform for many countries to re-visit their legislation and address the needs of regulating sensitive information in innovative ways.

Figure 7. Established legislation to protect privacy of digitized health-related data, by World Bank income group

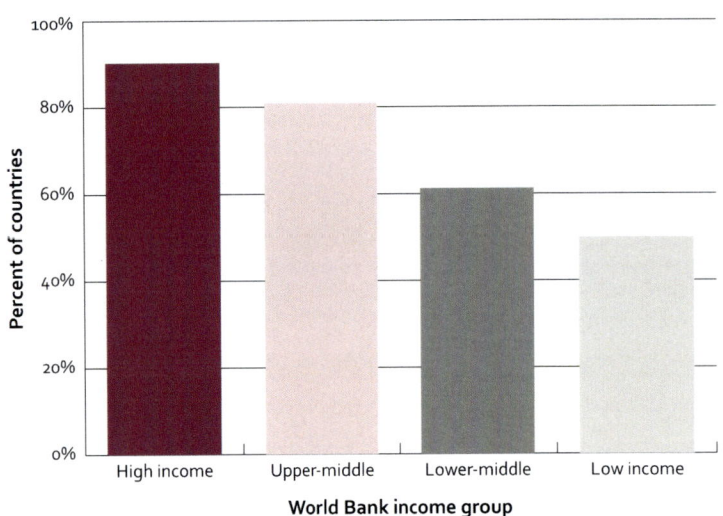

Figure 8. Established legislation to protect privacy of digitized health-related data, by WHO region

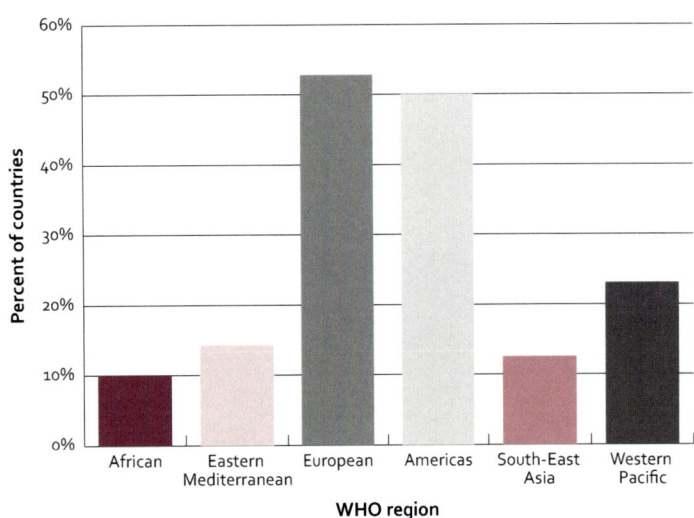

Discussion

From the data in Figures 6 through 8 it could be suggested that the human rights of patients whose data are stored electronically are not being duly respected in a large number of countries; only one third of responding countries currently protect the privacy of data held in an EHR. One explanation for this might be the relative immaturity of eHealth and EHRs. It was noted above that only a small number of countries use such electronic means of data processing at a high or very high level; it may be then that for all the main stakeholders (regulators, health-care professionals, and patients) general medical laws which regulate the relationship of trust between the doctor and the patient are deemed to be sufficient to cover the rather low level of electronic data processing which occurs at present.

The literature on current use of EHR in those regions of the world which report a wider general use of electronic data storage (The European and Americas Regions) would suggest that there is still only a limited use of fully integrated and interoperable EHRs. The *New England Journal of Medicine* reported in 2009 *(53)*, for example, that while 17% of United States hospitals use computerized provider-order entry for medications, only 1.5% have a comprehensive electronic records system (i.e. present in all clinical units), and an additional 7.6% have a basic system (i.e. present in at least one clinical unit). A survey published in the same journal on physicians' use of EHRs found in 2008 that 13% reported having a basic system in place, and only 4% of physicians reported having an extensive, fully functional electronic-records system *(54)*.

In Europe the situation is not much better, as shown in the 2011 eHealth Strategies Report *(55)* which showed that of 34 countries studied[4] only 7 had routinely deployed EHRs while 20 were still in the planning stage (the remainder being in early implementation or pilot stage). Given the still rather limited use of EHRs it is therefore understandable that the existing medical law framework of these countries, which has well-established rules on the duty of privacy owed by physicians and their co-workers to patients with respect to their medical information, is deemed sufficient to provide a good level of protection to patients.

It may also be however that the survey, in asking about legal rules to protect the privacy of patient information in EHRs, has resulted in evidence that only tells half the story. As noted in Section 1, privacy of medical records is protected not only by law but also by ethical conventions and social norms. The transposition of the core requirements of the Hippocratic Oath into national codes of conduct for health-care professionals is also a principal tool for protecting the interests of patients. Therefore it may be that, because the use of EHRs is in many countries still in its infancy, health-care professionals feel they have an adequate ethical framework for using these new tools. Indeed this was the finding of the eHealth Strategies Report which noted that in the early stages of using EHRs many countries simply squeeze the requirements of eHealth into existing legal rules, rather than drafting eHealth specific legislation:

> *Rarely does a country report on a coherent set of laws specifically designed to address these diverse aspects of eHealth. Rather, in most countries the use of eHealth is currently regulated only by the general legal framework, in particular by laws on patient rights and data protection and by regulations on professional conduct (55).*

---

4   The 34 countries studied were the 27 countries of the EU (with the 4 home countries of the United Kingdom counted separately as they each have their own health care systems therefore creating an EU number of 30), as well as the accession country Turkey and the 3 countries of the European Economic Area (Iceland, Norway, and Switzerland).

3.3 Legislation to regulate the sharing of health related data for patient care

Section 1 discussed that trust is a key element of the doctor-patient relationship. It noted that the nature and quality of the trust relationship is changing as health care evolves from a series of one-to-one and face-to-face relationships to a series of parallel collaborative relationships which may include remote and virtual consultations.

Given the importance of the possibility of sharing information across boundaries, whether institutional or geographic, the survey sought to examine the extent to which responding countries had addressed the privacy implications of sharing health related data. The object was to establish if a suitable legal framework existed to take eHealth to its next logical step – moving care beyond single institutions – and how far use of that framework was being made. Accordingly, respondents were asked a series of questions to establish how far the legislative frameworks governing their health care systems have been adjusted to allow sharing of information between health-care professionals within an organization, across organizations, and across national borders.

In order to better understand how far these issues had been legally embraced, the respondents were asked three linked questions.

Does your country have legislation which provides for the sharing of health-related data between health care staff through an EHR:

- *Within the same health care entity and its associated network of care providers?*
- *With different health care entities in your country?*
- *With health care entities in other countries?*

Key trends

- Globally the trend in adoption of special legislation to provide a framework for sharing information between health-care professionals is still low, with only one in four respondents globally stating they had such legislation.
- High-income countries in the European and the Americas Regions are the most likely to have legislation to cover data exchanges between health-care professionals both within an institution and between institutions in their countries.
- The legal framework for exchange of information between countries is almost non-existent with only 11% globally having such legislation and then primarily in European and the Americas Regions.

Results

Before reviewing the answers to the questions on legal frameworks for sharing data, it is useful to put the answers into context by referring again to the answers provided on the topic of patient information management. Here respondents were asked if data were held on paper or electronically, and if the latter whether those files could be transmitted electronically.

The data in Figure 5 show that many countries hold at least some patient medical data electronically, and that a significant number report the capacity to transmit those data electronically. Figures 9 and 10 show those data across WHO regions and by World Bank income group.

Figure 9. Formats of patient information in local health care facilities, by WHO region

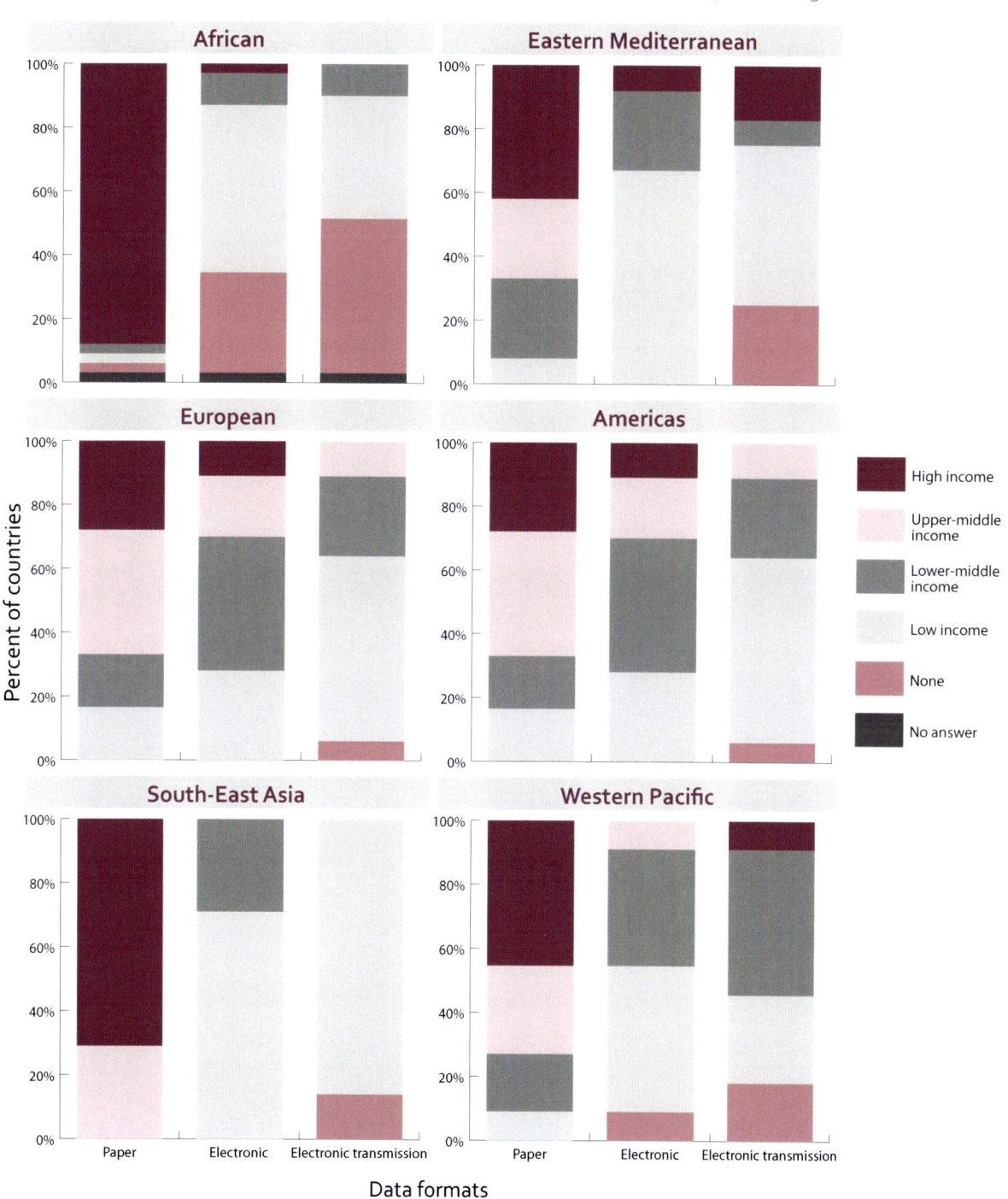

Figure 10. Formats of patient information in local health care facilities, by World Bank income group

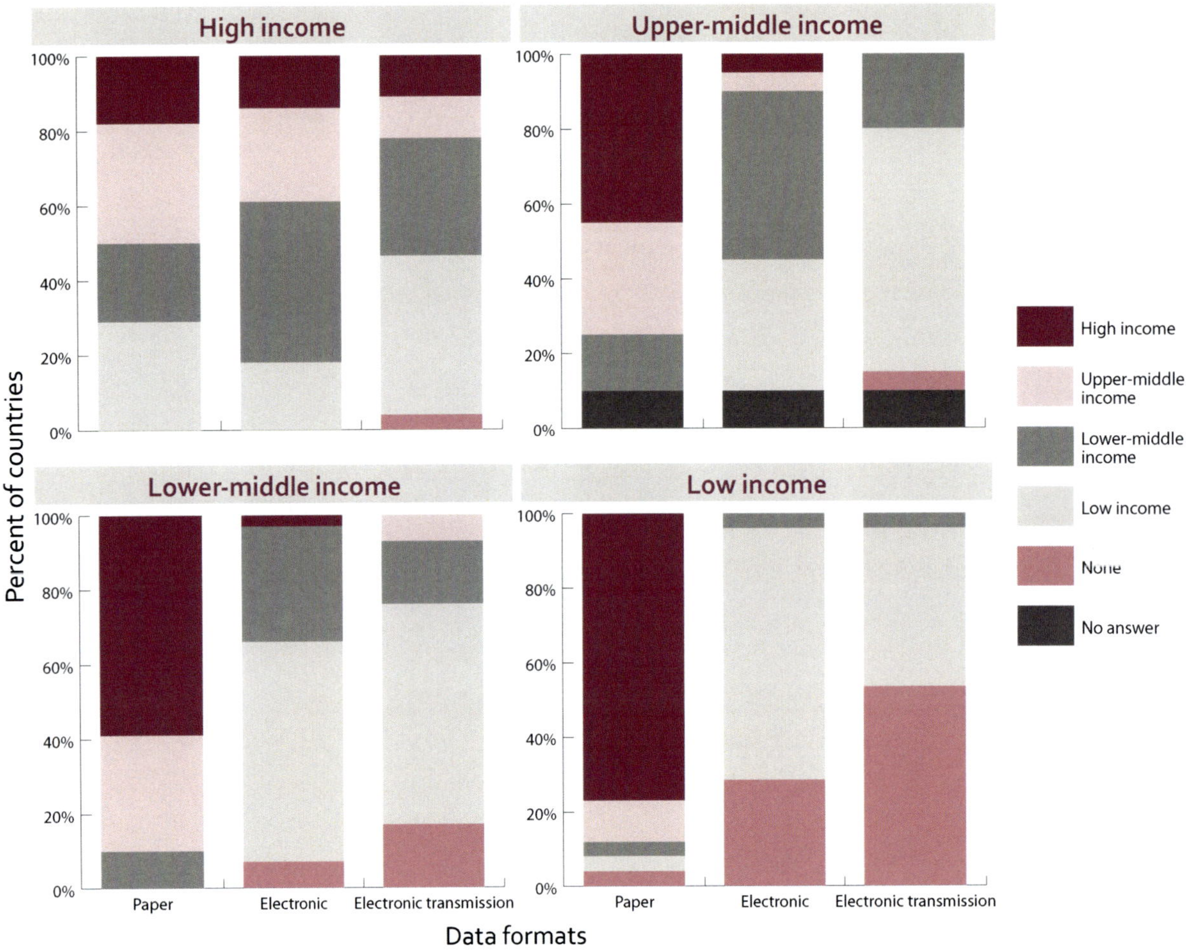

It is noteworthy that only the African Region has a significant number of responding countries reporting that they hold no electronic patient data (31%). Regions with higher-income countries all reported using at least some level of electronic transmission of data, although interestingly only a minority (22%) of them reported a high or very high usage of such transmission. It would seem therefore that while the use of electronic data storage is reasonably well-established, electronic data transmission is still in early stages of adoption.

Figure 11. Legislation on sharing health-related data (through an EHR) within the same health facility, globally

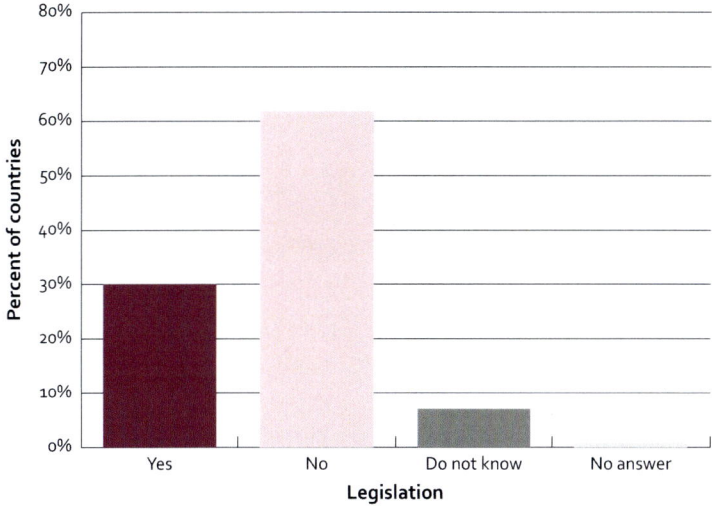

Figure 12. Legislation on sharing health-related data (through an EHR) within the same health facility, by World Bank income group

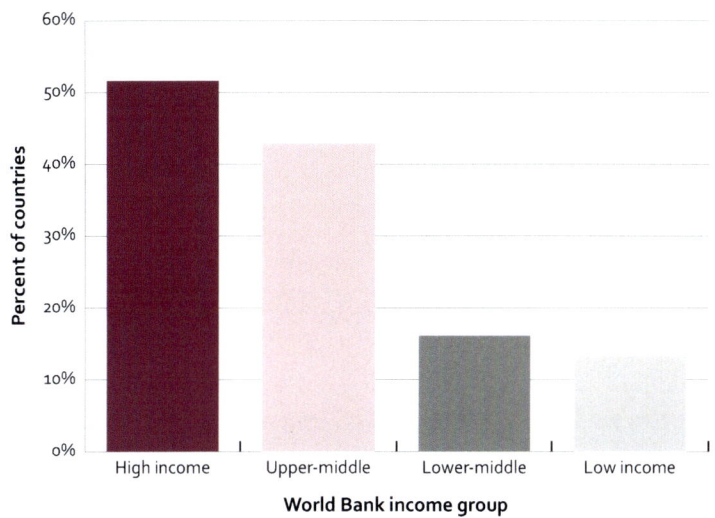

Figure 13. Legislation on sharing health-related data (through an EHR) within the same health facility, by WHO region

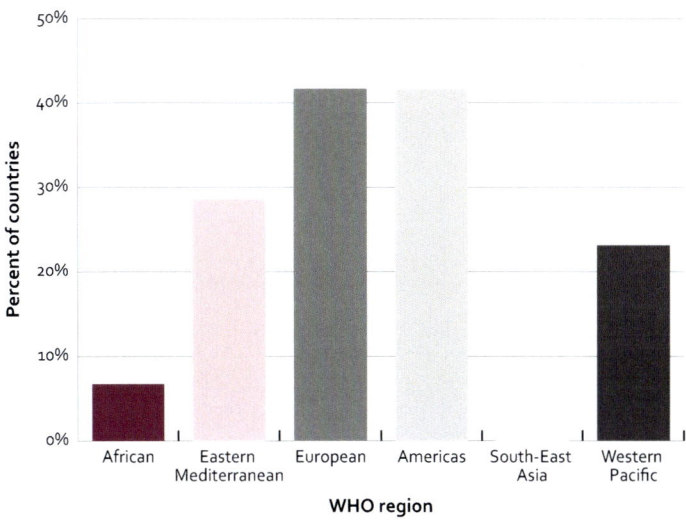

The global positive response rate to the question was not high; only 26% of all responding countries stated that they had any legislation in place specifically addressing health-related data transfer between health-care professionals within an organization (Figure 11); 23% had legislation to cover sharing between organizations (Figure 14); and only 11% globally reported having legislation to cover sharing of EHRs across national borders (Figure 15).

Figure 14. Global statistics showing legislation on sharing EHRs between heath care facilities within the country

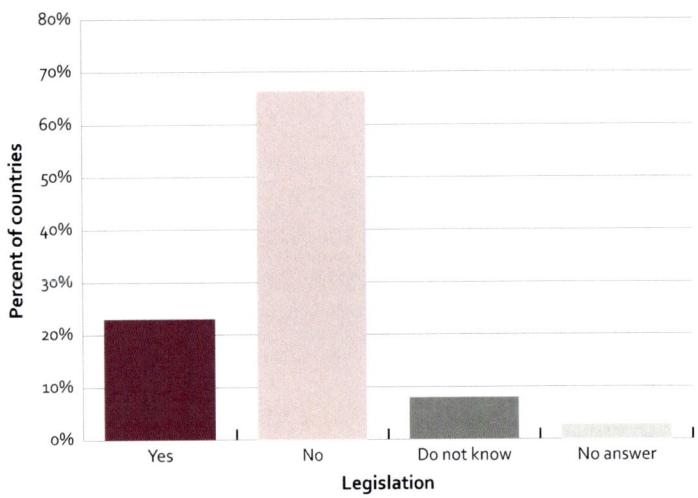

Figure 15. Global statistics showing legislation on sharing EHRs with health care facilities in other countries

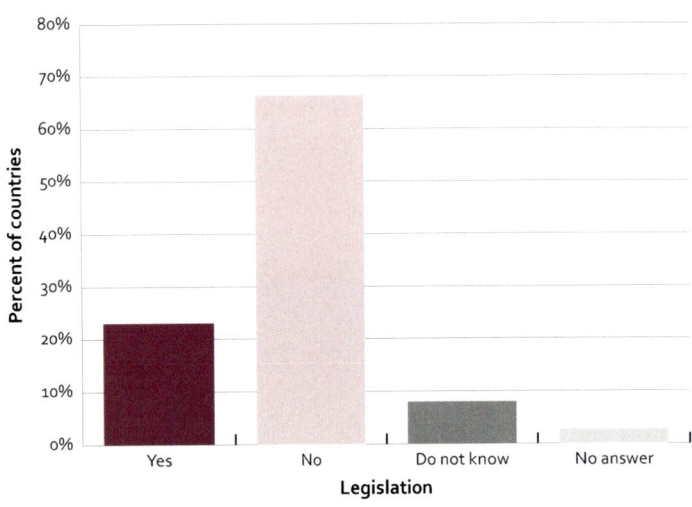

These figures demonstrate quite starkly that few countries have found it expedient to develop specific legal frameworks for data sharing, which may be considered as somewhat surprising given that some 88% of the respondents to the survey also reported using some form of electronic storage of information, and that 77% of the respondents globally use some form of electronic transfer of such information, even though very few do so to a significant extent.

When reviewed by WHO region and World Bank income group, however, it is evident that in those countries which have already invested heavily in eHealth infrastructure and who report a high to medium level of electronic transfer of patient data, a better level of such legislation is found (Figures 12 and 13). It would seem then that here again the lack of regulation can be seen as matter of maturity of the applications area. It may be that until the medical use case for routine sharing of EHRs within and between health care organizations has been accepted by key stakeholders in health care systems, the necessary impetus to adapt the legal frameworks simply will not exist.

The figures demonstrate a generally good correlation between those countries reporting a very high, high, or medium level of electronic transmission of individual patient data held in local health facilities and those countries having specific legislation to regulate such transfers. The exception would seem to be in the lower-middle income countries where seven countries (24% of the region) (Figure 10) report a high to medium level of electronic transmission of data, but where only two (6.5%) of the same respondents report having legislation in place to accommodate such transfer.

Generally however, it is fair to say that those regions that have an extensive use of EHRs have started to address the need for a legal framework to ensure that such transfer is done according to legal principles. In a further survey it would be very interesting to analyse all such legislation in detail to establish the extent to which it covered administrative issues, such as health-care professional accreditation, and how it seeks to address the day-to-day work flow issues of sharing information.

The trend is also evident in the survey results from the second question in this series, which asked respondents if legislation frameworks existed for sharing data between institutions in the home country (Figures 16 and 17). Findings show only a very small variation from the data in Figures 12 and 13.

Figure 16. Legislation on sharing EHRs between heath care facilities within the country, by World Bank income group

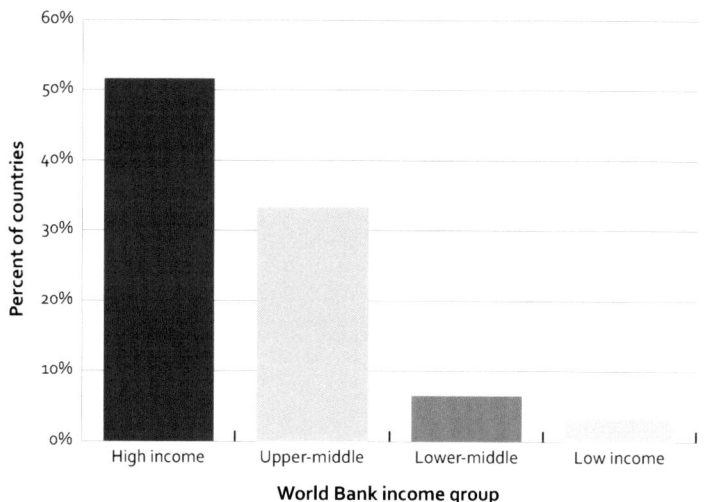

Figure 17. Legislation on sharing EHRs between heath care facilities within the country, by WHO region

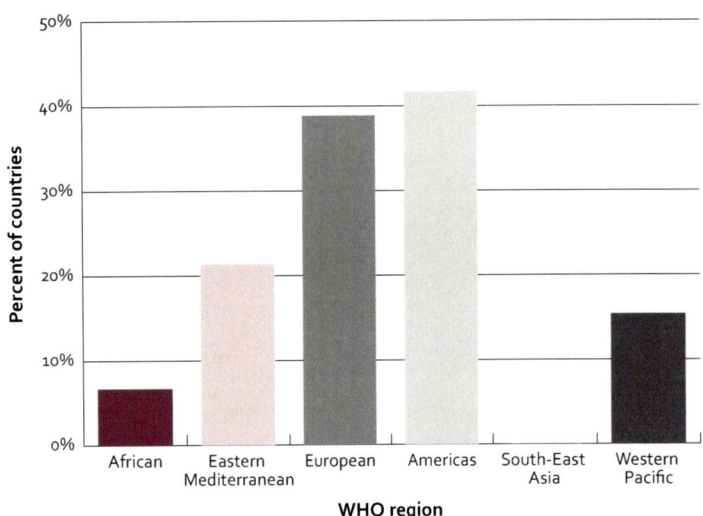

The picture is very different indeed when considering the legal framework for sharing information across national borders (Figures 18 and 19). It is worth noting that globally only 11% (12 countries) reported having such legislation in place (Figure 15). A breakdown of those figures by region identified only a small group of countries within the WHO Regions of the Americas and Europe which have addressed the need for such legislation.

It would seem then that despite considerable discussion on medical tourism *(56)*, and outsourcing of medical service across borders, little has been done on a legislative level to accommodate such transfer of data, particularly outside of high-income countries.

Figure 18. Legislation on sharing EHRs with health care facilities in other countries, by World Bank income group

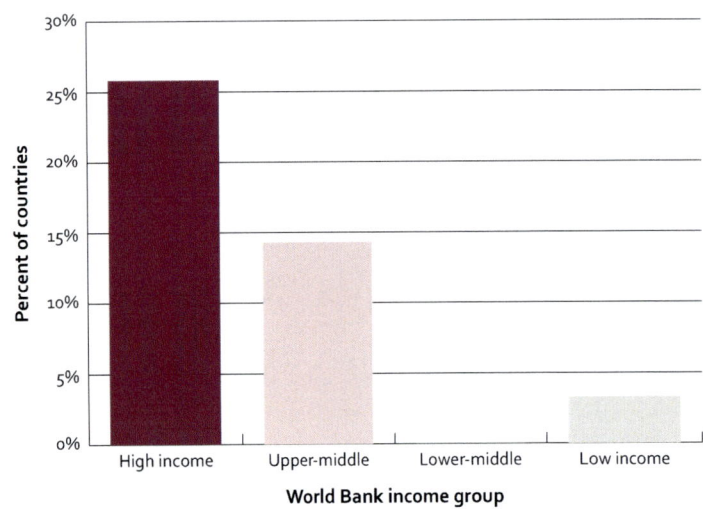

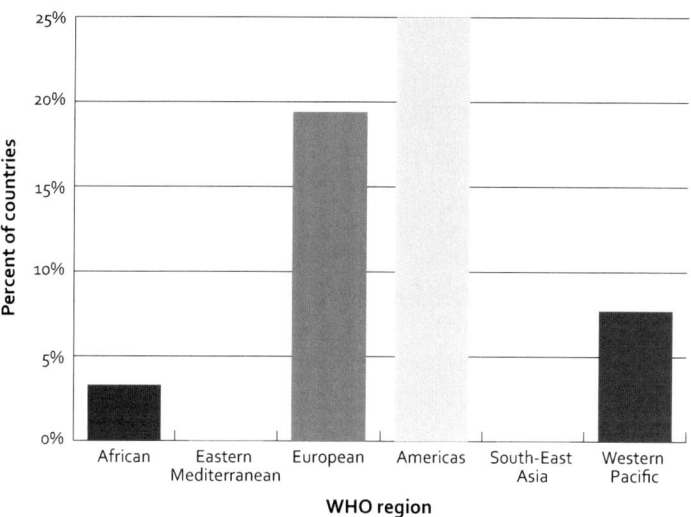

Figure 19. Legislation on sharing EHRs with health care facilities in other countries, by WHO region

Discussion

There are two ways of interpreting these data – one positive and one less so. From a positive point of view it can be noted that in countries where a significant investment has been made in establishing the technological infrastructure for moving away from paper records to electronic records, roughly a quarter have also adopted a relevant legal framework to facilitate the sharing of such records within and between institutions of their home countries, which would indicate that the right path has been adopted. This would however also suggest that the general mode of adopting eHealth legislation is retrospective: investments are made first in technology and infrastructure and then legislation is adapted or adopted once use cases have been established. The data would also suggest that such adoption is slow. Furthermore, given that approximately 25% of countries reported they have a medium, high, or very high level of electronic transmission of data, it is worrying that a significant number must be making such transmissions without an adequate legal framework to protect the privacy of that information.

When reviewing the data more negatively, however, and focusing on the sharing of data across national borders, one sees a low level of legal response. Despite a wide range of research projects and policies setting out the benefits of cross-border health care and eHealth tools to facilitate the sharing of medical expertise between nations and jurisdictions, little has been done to ensure that such sharing of data is supported by an appropriate legal framework. It is disheartening, although perhaps not surprising, to note that despite the significant investments made in eHealth technology around the world – e.g. complex national systems such as that adopted in England through Connecting for Health and private initiatives in mHealth (Mobile Health) being operated in many of the lower-income countries, that so little has been done to accommodate transfer of data between entities and countries through legislation.

The EU offers a very good case study of this conundrum. For more than 20 years the EU has been funding research and developing policy in the field of eHealth. The history of these endeavours is neatly summarized into three phases in a briefing paper of the European Health Telematics Association (EHTEL) entitled *The three ages of eHealth (57)*. The paper highlights the first age of eHealth in the EU as starting in 1989 when the first EU research budget for eHealth was adopted. At this time eHealth was known as

Advance Informatics in Medicine and concentrated on developing computer technology for use in health care – notably imaging. In the 1990s the focus sharpened and the next research programme, which ran from 1991–1994, concentrated its efforts on the development of networks and tools for health-care professionals. In the latter half of the decade the Telematics Applications for Health Programme (1994–1998) focused on continuity of care, particularly the user's needs. It was at this stage that the EU adopted its Data Protection Directive and although there were very few people working directly on eHealth law at this stage, the first conference papers and publications on the application of data protection law in health telematics started to appear *(58, 59)*.

Yet despite the fact that more than ten years have passed since scholars, policy-makers, and those charged with actually delivering health care using eHealth tools have started to question the appropriateness of the existing legal frameworks for using these tools, very little real progress has been made. The extent of work still needed in Europe alone has been made evident in the a large-scale pilot project named epSOS – Smart Open Services for European Patients.[5]

The epSOS large-scale pilot focuses on electronic patient record systems and operates within a complex policy environment. The initial focus is on cross-border access to patient summary data sets and electronic prescriptions. The exchange of data, which lies at the heart of the epSOS pilot, requires trust between all parties. The project has sought to foster trust to ensure that health-care professionals can rely upon the authenticity of the clinical data on which they will base decisions; that suitable systems of security exist to ensure that data cannot be accessed by unauthorized parties; and that patient rights of informed consent to data access are duly respected by all parties (authenticity, integrity, and confidentiality). However, the 22 participating countries in Europe did not have a sufficiently developed legal framework to allow such transfer. Accordingly the exchange of data in epSOS, at least in the initial stages of the pilot, has had to be based on a series of contracts and memoranda of understanding.

It may be argued therefore that at present there is not sufficient legal maturity at national or international level to really facilitate cross-border sharing of medical data in order to facilitate either better patient care for patients or to enable research. It is to be hoped however that the EU will soon lead the way at least in terms of creating greater legal certainty to share medical information for cross-border care of its citizens based on the European legislation on Patients' Rights in Cross-Border Healthcare adopted in 2011 *(44)*. The legislation establishes the framework for European citizens to seek care in any EU Member State regardless of their country of usual residence. The Directive foresees eHealth as a core element of such care provision and has required Member States to adopt common interoperability standards to allow the transfer of health related data between EU Member States. It is interesting to note that this 2011 legislation talks expressly about the interests of patients in accessing their records and provides for the adoption of interoperability standards to allow the sharing of records, but does not mention the concept of ownership of the record. The key issue in terms of patients' rights is access and control, not a property right of ownership.

---

5   www.epsos.eu

3.4 Legislation on patient access and the control of EHRs

It was noted in the literature review that as health care has evolved in the past century the idea that the patient has a direct interest in the health care record has developed. Until relatively recently the concept of patient privacy was covered by the ideas in the Hippocratic Oath, which essentially required that health-care professionals maintain secrecy, rather than any concepts of rights of patients to access their own records and control access of others. To a large extent this was because when records were held only in a paper format, written by hand by a doctor on paper owned by a doctor there was a strong sense that the record was in fact owned by the doctor. With the advent of EHRs, where the ownership of the medium on which the record is captured is less important, and where the record itself is composed of a wide range of data items originating from a wide variety of sources, the concept of record ownership is less clear.

In order to establish how far the global health community had adopted ideas of patients' rights to access and control their health care records, the survey posed a series of questions about such rights starting with a simple question on whether a right of access exists. This was followed with four more detailed questions about patients' control of the EHR:

- *Does your country have legislation which allows individuals to demand their health-related data be corrected when held in an EHR if they know it is inaccurate?*
- *Does your country have legislation which allows individuals to demand the deletion of personal data and/or health-related data from their EHR?*
- *If 'yes', will the deletion of data leave a trace on the EHR which will be visible to health-care professionals treating that person in the future?*
- *Do individuals have the legal right to specify which health-related data from their EHR can be shared with health provider(s) of their choice?*

Key trends

- Globally the adoption of legislation which gives express rights to patients to access their health care record are still low – but absolutely in line with the number that have adopted legislation which expressly addresses the privacy of the EHR.
- Most of the countries adopting such legislation are in the World Bank high-income group.
- Lower-middle and low-income countries appear to be less advanced in giving such rights to patients.
- Rights on correction are broadly in line with rights to access, but rights to deletion are very limited, with only very few countries allowing deletion with trace.
- Rights to control who may access a record by name or professional role are also limited.

Results

The global figures show that 28% of countries have adopted legislation that grants patients access to their records, while 63% have not done so, and 8% reported 'do not know' (Figure 20). These numbers are absolutely in line with the responses to question 6.3 in which 30% globally reported they had adopted legislation on EHR privacy and 63% reported that they had not done so. It would seem then to be relatively encouraging that once EHR legislation has been adopted a certain level of control over that information is given to patients.

Figure 20. Legislation granting individuals the right to access their EHR, globally

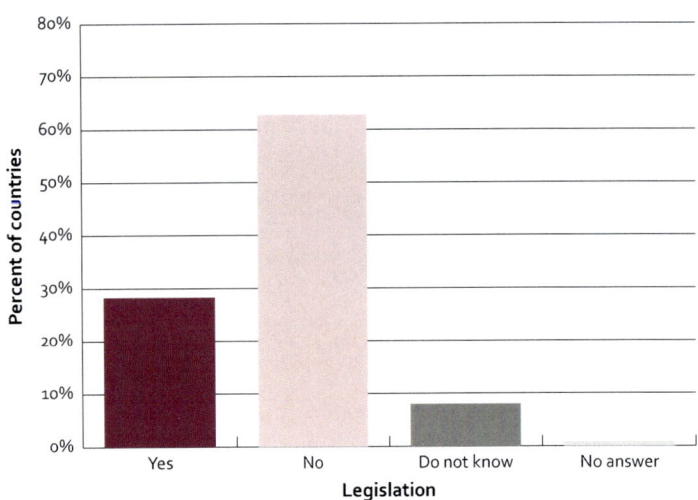

Figures 21 and 22 show the responses to the question about individual access to EHRs. The positive response rate of 56% in the European Region can be accounted for largely by European Union Member States that have interpreted the duty contained in Article 12 of the Data Protection Directive to mean that patients should have access to their records. The Directive requires only that Member States shall guarantee every data subject the right to obtain from the controller of data without constraint, at reasonable intervals and without excessive delay or expense:

- confirmation as to whether or not data relating to him are being processed and information at least as to the purposes of the processing, the categories of data concerned, and the recipients or categories of recipients to whom the data are disclosed;

- communication to him in an intelligible form of the data undergoing processing and of any available information as to their source.

From the wording of these clauses it can be seen that access to the record as such is not required, which will account for why a number of countries in the EU have responded negatively to the question in the survey.

Figure 21. Legislation granting individuals the right to access their EHR, by World Bank income group

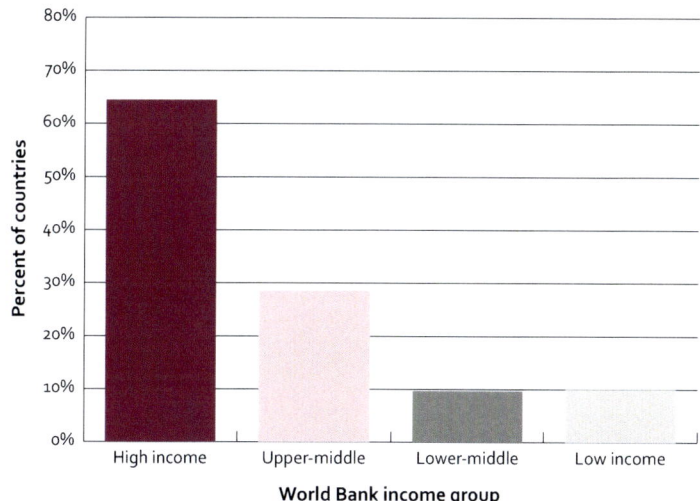

Figure 22. Legislation granting individuals the right to access their EHR, by WHO region

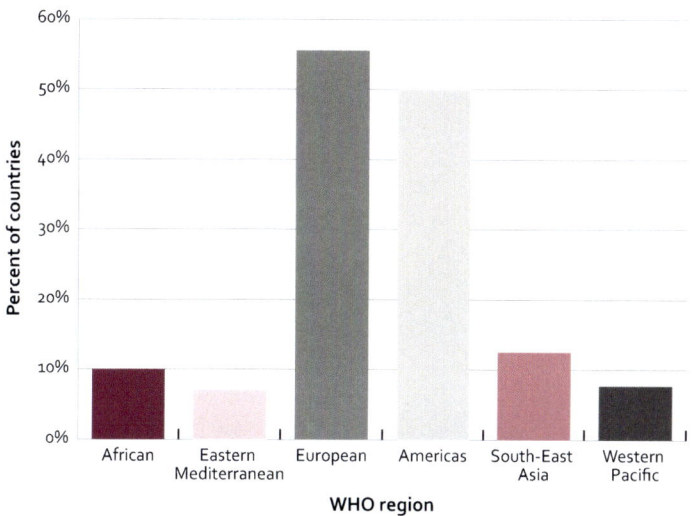

The survey went on to look more closely at the nature of rights that were granted to individuals, asking if patients had a right to seek correction and deletion of elements of the record and if deletion was permitted, the fact that a deletion had occurred was visible on the face of the record (Figures 23 and 24).

Figure 23. Legislation allowing individuals to request inaccuracies of their health-related data be corrected within an EHR, by World Bank income group

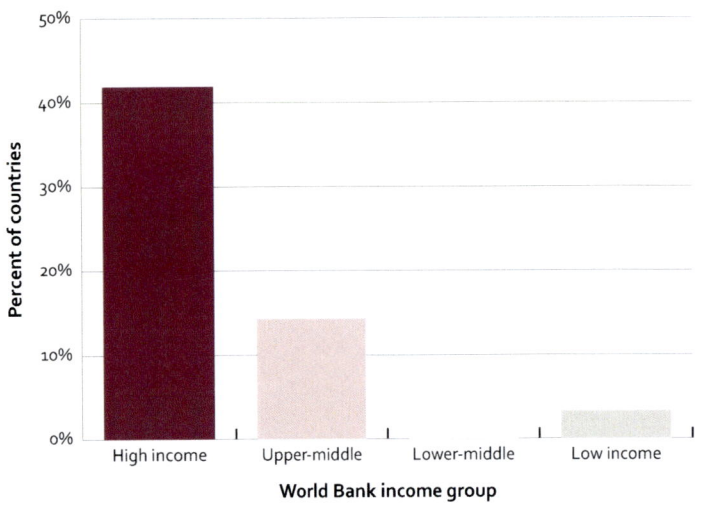

Figure 24. Legislation allowing individuals to request inaccuracies of their health-related data be corrected within an EHR, by WHO region

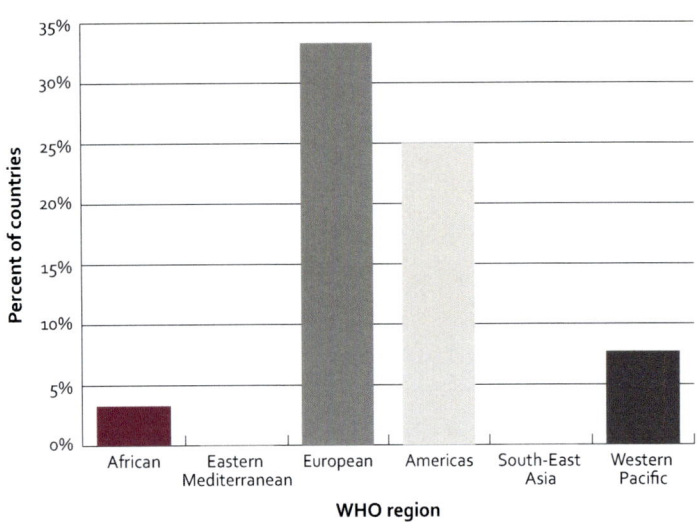

The data in Figures 23 and 24 demonstrate that rights to correction are broadly in line with the rights to access, although this right is not as widely protected. On the right to make deletions, however, the numbers drop dramatically. Only 17 countries reported that a right to deletion existed, and of those just under half allowed such deletion to leave no trace on the record (Tables 1 and 2).

Table 1. Legislation allowing individuals the right to request deletion of data (with and without trace) from their EHR, by World Bank income group

Number of 'yes' responses by World Bank income group	High income	Upper-middle income	Lower-middle income	Low income
Right to delete	13	3	0	1
Delete w/o trace	5	2	0	1
Number of countries	31	21	31	30

Table 2. Legislation allowing individuals the right to request deletion of data (with and without trace) from their EHR, by WHO region

Number of 'yes' responses by WHO region	African	Eastern Mediterranean	European	Americas	South-East Asia	Western Pacific
Right to delete	1	0	12	3	0	1
Delete w/o trace	1	0	5	2	0	0
Number of countries	30	14	36	12	8	13

The majority of countries, 70% globally, do not allow the patient to demand any form of deletion in the health record. There may be many reasons for this. First, it may be that other legal rules forbid deletion, since it is a common requirement of health care systems that the record is a complete account of all aspects of the patient's interaction with the health care system. Rules of professional regulation, as well as potential legal proceedings, mean that the record must be complete and so deletion may not be allowed. The low rate of acceptance of a right of deletion may also have its roots deep in the history of the health record, where the record was seen as the property of the doctor and where a patient might have rights to see the records, but where the patient has no legitimate rights to interfere in the property of the doctor. The discussion below highlights the impact of these constructions and questions whether granting patients the right to delete parts of the record is important for the advancement of eHealth.

The final question in the survey related directly to patients' rights with respect to the use of EHR; it asked if patients had a right to specify who could access an EHR (e.g. only named health-care professionals or classes of health-care professionals). Here the results correlate strongly with results on correction and deletion. While a patient is reasonably frequently granted a right to see the record and know what is recorded, in most cases the patient does not have a right to control who may have access to the record (Figure 25).

Figure 25. Legislation giving individuals the right to specify with which health provider(s) to share their EHR, globally

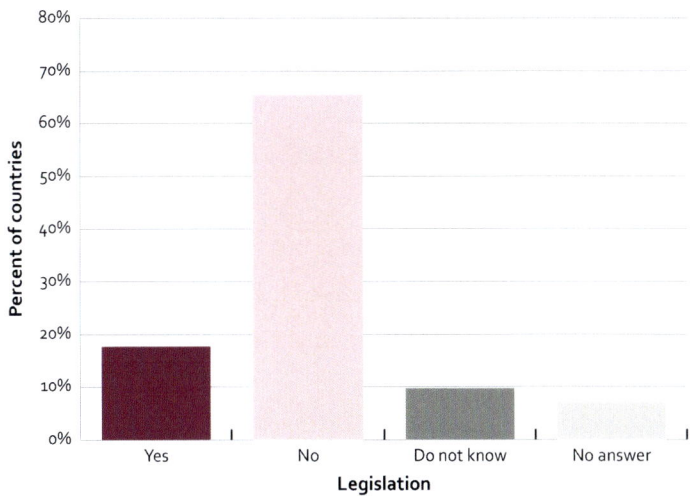

While globally 28% of responding countries gave a right to patients to access the record, 25% globally gave a right to correct, 18% gave a right to control who had access, and only 15% gave a right to delete. There is a clear linear progression in which a patient may be accorded some rights in knowing what is recoded about him or her, and correcting mistakes, but when one gets into the realm of control of the record (in terms of who can access it and what it contains), the rights remain with the health-care professional or health care system. It may be argued that this is based in a legal construction of ownership in which the record is still seen as the property the health-care professional or the system and where the patient may have human rights based interests in knowing what data is stored, but no potential to exercise rights which would imply a property interest in the record.

Discussion

With the advent of EHRs many countries have adopted legislation which gives the patient a greater level of control over the information. As a result a tension is now emerging between the interest of the patient in controlling information and the interests of the treating health-care professional in having access to a complete record of all relevant information. In some countries concern has arisen that the very tools which sought to provide access and increase patient autonomy might impact negatively on the quality of care a doctor can provide, and thus might be at odds with the doctor's duty of beneficence/non-maleficence.

Perhaps the most controversial issue here is the right accorded in some legislations of a patient to hide aspects of their medical record, which the survey results show has a very low level of uptake among responding countries, and where again the countries in the European Region lead in according this right.

The reason for this is that many European jurisdictions, in transposing the rights under the Data Protection Directive, have created a rule which allows patients to hide data. In some cases this includes the use of a virtual sealed envelope – a part of the record which is accessible to only named health-care professionals or health-care professionals with a prescribed clinical role. This method is used, for example, in England and Sweden where the system in place allows patients to specify who may have access to which information.

This method for granting greater autonomy to the patient can, however, have two detrimental effects. First, the existence of a sealed record may inadvertently create privacy issues, since the mere fact that the record flags that some information is not accessible indicates that highly sensitive information exists for that patient, which is a piece of personal data in itself (60). Second, in giving a patient the right to conceal certain information, not all health-care professionals have access to the complete record, which could compromise the health of the patient who has concealed information and could also impact negatively on the health of others. If, for example, a doctor is not aware of a diagnosis of a mental health condition he/she may prescribe inappropriate medication which could affect not only the health of the patient taking the medication but also the safety of people around the patient.

In order to address this the English National Health Service has adopted a 'seal and lock' approach. The 'lock' aspect means that no flag exists to show information is missing in the general record. However, as this may create a conflict between the individual's data protection rights and the National Health Service's duty of care to ensure relevant patient information is available to all treating health professionals, a further capacity to reveal (unlock) and unseal envelopes is built into the medical records software. Based on medical context and health-care professional accreditation the record will indicate that a sealed envelope exists and will allow certain certified professionals to unseal the envelope, with any such unsealing being recorded in a transaction trace, so that the patient could retrospectively see who had had access to information which he or she had wanted to keep private.

Interestingly, France has not added the step of revealing and unsealing into their EHR privacy responses; it created instead a system where patients can seal information in such a way that the existence of the sealed envelope is not visible to anyone and accordingly cannot be opened. The Social Security Finance Act of 19 December 2007 allows beneficiaries of National Health Insurance to manage both their personal medical record and provides for the right of the patient, or his/her legal representative, to make certain information in the record inaccessible. This concept – known in French as masquage du masquage (hiding of hiding) – has created a great deal of anxiety among health-care professionals, many of whom are very reluctant to use EHRs if they feel they do not represent a complete record of all the information they may need in order to best treat a patient *(61)*.

The experiences of the National Health Service in England and France thus highlight the technical problems which arise when a health care system seeks to give greater data control to patients over their EHRs. It is therefore highly understandable that many nations have not yet embraced tools and laws which allow patients to exercise greater control over their EHRs. However, the fact that the baseline is in place – globally 28% of countries grant rights of access (65% of high-income countries do so) – suggests that globally greater patient control of EHRs is emerging. It is therefore important that the experiences of countries such as France and England are shared widely so that countries may learn from them, and so that patients' rights can be balanced with wider public interests and health-care professionals' interest more effectively.

3.5 EHRs for research

The literature review (Section 2) made clear that a certain value exists in EHRs not only for the treatment of patients, but also for the development of medical care and wider medical research. The EHR, and indeed a range of other eHealth applications such as remote monitoring devices, offer a wealth of information which could be a major support to health related research. Some scholars have even argued that they offer such a major potential contribution that it would be unethical not to explore them, Hoffmann and Podgurski *(62)* argue, for example, that the transition from paper medical files to electronic health records provides an unprecedented potential to drive significant advances in medical knowledge, but that this potential can be fully realized only if the data available to researchers is representative of the patient population as a whole. Thus, allowing individual patients to exclude their health information, in keeping with traditional notions of privacy controlled by informed consent, may compromise the research enterprise and the medical benefits it produces.

Some countries have addressed this challenge by providing legislation that will allow the sharing of identifiable patient data without the patient's consent. An example of this is the 2001 Health and Social Care Act in England which provides for the use of anonymized data for research purposes and also addresses the possibility of using identifiable data without patient consent in certain circumstances when research is in the public interest. Parliament has provided for a legal power to ensure that patient identifiable information currently needed to support essential health care activity can be used without the consent that should normally be obtained, where there is no reasonably practicable alternative. Such health care activity may include preventive medicine, medical diagnosis, medical research, provision of care, and treatment and management of health and social care services.

The use of anonymized data for research was not addressed by the survey per se; instead it focused on the extent to which existing legal responses had addressed the potential of using identifiable EHR data in cross-border research. Such legislation may of course be based on patient consent or on other privacy control measures. The point of the question was to establish if international research issues had been addressed, based on the principle that international research is legal, the most complex to regulate, and that therefore if this area had been addressed it would be a good indicator of addressing the research potential of EHRs in general. The question was:

Does your country have legislation which allows for the transmission and sharing of research data containing personal and health-related data between research entities in different countries?

Key trends

- Globally, the issue of access to EHR data for research purposes has not been regulated widely yet; the majority of responding nations have not addressed this in any way.

Results

Globally, the responses on allowing personally identifiable health-related data to be used for international research purposes showed that this has simply not been addressed by the majority of legislatures yet, with over 70% reporting that no such legislation existed (Figure 26).

Figure 26. Legislation allowing personally-identifiable health data to be used for international research purposes

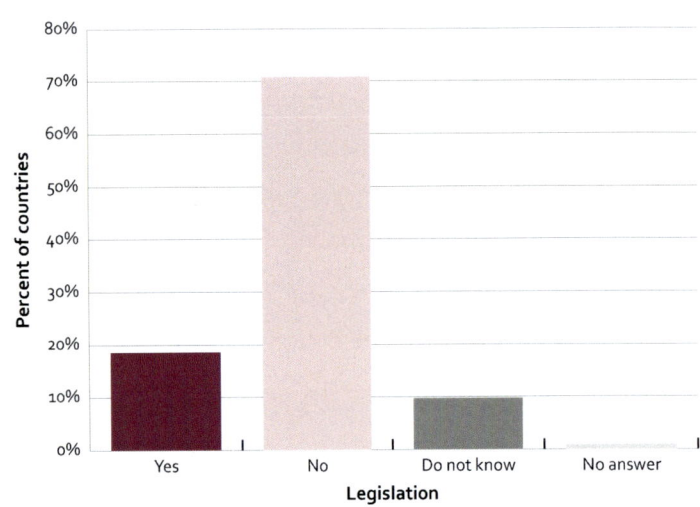

Discussion

The results shown in Figure 26 may fail to highlight the core issue in the use of EHR based data for research, as it asked about use of identifiable data for international research generally and may therefore not have concentrated the respondents minds on the use of data in EHRs. Moreover, it asked specifically about international research, not the extent to which local research using EHRs is permitted.

The literature suggests, however, that there will be little variation between allowing EHRs to be used locally or internationally, at least where international research is between countries with established co-research records. The literature also suggests that the preoccupation of the legislators is not in control of how research is conducted, but on whether research using nominative or identifiable data should be allowed at all. One of the few countries that have so far really grappled with this issue is the USA. The HITECH rules (outlined in Box 2), are one of the first examples of legislation which addresses the power held within EHRs to drive research.

These rules are, however, not entirely focused on privacy. In line with the ethical 'bargain' described in Chapter 2.1, HITECH seeks to ensure that EHRs can be put to good use to treat patients both as individuals and in terms of patients in general by promoting health sciences research. The rules provide that HIPAA-covered entities and their business associates may not share data without the consent of the patient unless such sharing is for the treatment of the individual, for public health activities *(63)* or for research *(64)*. While the HIPAA privacy rule provides that de-identified data may be shared freely for research and sets out 18 data categories which must be eliminated in order to render a record de-identified (these include obvious items like name, address, and full date of birth) *(65)*, the HITECH legislation expands this exception by providing that identifiable data may be shared without consent so long as it is not sold at profit by the data holder. Any price charged for transfer of identifiable data should reflect only the costs of preparation and transmittal of the data for research. It is in this last exception that a balance is struck between privacy of the individual and the interests in sharing data for research as a matter of general public interest.

The objective of this exception is essentially to unlock the power of EHRs for research. Evans *(66)* argues that records-based research with patient consent can create an undue burden on the patient and can also lead to bias. She notes that a core element of the HITECH legislation is to avoid cases where a lack of records-based research potentially places other human beings at risk. The HITECH legislation may therefore be seen as a significant opportunity to come to terms with the collective nature of knowledge generation in a world where large-scale records research is set to play a more prominent role. The USA is unusual in having taking this bold step to ensure that EHR data may be more easily unlocked for research; most other countries do not (yet) provide that such data may be released for research purposes without the express consent of the patient.

On the value of EHRs as a research tool Hoffmann and Podgurski *(62)* suggest, that when studies involve electronic record review rather than human experimentation, the traditional, autonomy-dominated model should give way to one that emphasizes the common good. In record-based studies, the limited benefits of individual informed consent come at too high a cost – difficult administrative burdens, significant expenses, and a tendency to create selection biases that distort study outcomes. Although it is not uniformly accepted, there is an emerging trend in legislative responses to recognize that while consent is an absolute requirement for any research involving physically or psychologically invasive investigations, where research studies involve only record review, it is appropriate to turn to the value of the common good as a counterweight to concern about individual risk *(62)*.

4 Conclusions

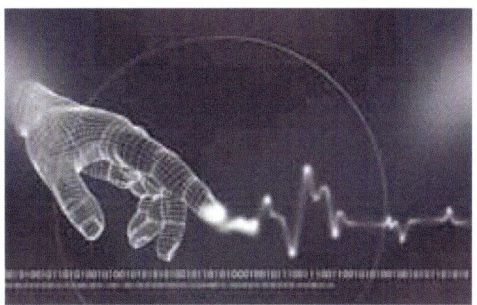

The analysis of the responses given to questions on the legal protection of the privacy of the EHR shows two clear trends. First, a reasonably high level of legal protection of the general privacy of health related information exists. In the majority of countries surveyed, however, legislation has not been highly developed beyond the common human rights of privacy of home, family, and communication. Second, the number of countries adopting more specific eHealth related privacy protection legislation is still low. The trend clearly indicates, however, that as use of EHRs increases, regulatory frameworks become more robust and legislative changes are made to ensure that privacy in the EHR is maintained.

Such a reactive mode of law-making is unfortunate, though understandable. While legal safeguards provided under general rules of privacy may be sufficient for the institutionally based use of EHRs which is common at present, it is doubtful that it will be sufficient to build public confidence in the sort of widespread use of advanced EHRs that many countries identify as the basis of health care systems designed for the 21st century – systems that seek to evolve from sickness management to wellness services, an approach which will be needed as populations age, and the numbers of people requiring long-term care grow.

- Generally good levels of basic rights to information privacy exist globally.

- Specific health information privacy protection is not as widely present and is often contained in professional codes of conduct rather than law.

- Legislation specifically aimed at protecting privacy in EHRs is limited to countries where considerable deployment of EHRs already exists.

The uptake of advanced eHealth tools needs a supportive legal environment. While many recent reports show a considerable openness to the concept of EHRs and other eHealth tools *(67, 52)*, it is widely believed that patients are not yet satisfied that their privacy is adequately protected in such systems. Wynia and Dunne note, for example, that far and away the most commonly recognized ethical barrier to using EHRs is the lack of assurance of privacy and the perceived risk of security breaches, since not all parties interested in EHRs have the same level of legal or ethical obligations to respect patient privacy *(68)*. Public education campaigns which set out the privacy-related rights and duties of the parties would also be a helpful addition to addressing this unease on the part of patients.

The key leanings from the survey and the literature therefore lead to recommendations to legislators on two axes: building trust in the EHR; and maximizing its use for patient care and wider public health.

- Laws and regulations on the use of EHRs tend to be reactive; few states use legislation as a tool to facilitate and drive uptake of EHRs.

- Few initiatives have been adopted to place EHR privacy legislation in an actionable context of rigorous clinical and information governance systems.

4.1 Building trust

Privacy and trust are inextricably linked in health care.[6] The nature of the relationship between the patient and the provider of care is necessarily one of trust in which the patient provides his or her information to the health-care professional, either orally or through laboratory tests and other physical investigations, and trusts that the health-care provider will use that information in order to provide help and treatment. In legal terms this is a simple fiduciary relationship in which the consumer has a right to expect that a professional works to a high professional standard commensurate to the trust placed in him or her.

The analysis and discussion in this report make evident that the limits of this sort of simple fiduciary trust relationship in health care have been reached. Health care is much more complex now than it was 100 years ago and treatments require much more detailed information about a patient, and may include very wide-reaching information such as genetic data that can predict future health states. Health care systems also are much more complex; today the care of a patient can require expertise from many more people and organizations, which implies the need to share information across groups. The patient has also become much more closely involved in his or her care. Not only does the Internet bring scientific medical knowledge to anyone's computer screen, but health care systems expect patients to be more engaged – to understand the implications of obesity and avoid it; to know their cholesterol level and actively manage it; and in some countries to assess health care options and make active choices on care. The questions therefore arise: Are the current legal frameworks adequate to allow health information to flow appropriately in this new construction of health care? Is the level of privacy protection in health care good enough to build the trust of the patient in sharing his or her information? WHO Member States have clearly recognized the potential of legal frameworks to build trust in simple one-to-one health care relationships; the time has come now to use law much more proactively to build trust in the new information rich systems which are emerging. The bullet points above provide a basis from which such actions may be addressed in order to establish law as a key facilitator to drive greater adoption of eHealth.

- Adaptations should be made to existing legal frameworks to ensure that data can be shared appropriately to provide patient care and support wider public health initiatives.

- Patient trust should be built by giving patients more information about how their data are handled and providing education on the technical and regulatory requirement of privacy and security which are used to ensure that data are shared appropriately.

- Health-care professional engagement in use of EHRs for better health care delivery should be facilitated by clearer legal guidelines on rights and duties.

- Public trust in the privacy of EHRs should be built by publishing the results of privacy impact assessments conducted by trusted third parties.

---

6   For an interesting discussion on how trust in eHealth systems can be built through more refined privacy legislation, see the position paper of COCIR "On the Privacy and Protection of Health Data" at www.cocir.org

4.2 Making data work: expanding the uses of EHRs

Privacy in health care is complex; it necessarily involves the balancing of interests of individuals against interests of society a whole. The power of shareable data in providing better care for patients would seem to be well understood in the literature (69) and is even beginning to make an appearance in political statements – the EU pilot on shareable summary records and electronic prescriptions is built on an understanding that EHRs should be accessible worldwide. So, for example, if a citizen with diabetes and a penicillin allergy is involved in a car crash outside his or her home country the health-care professional in the foreign country will be able to provide safer and more efficient care if he/she knows about these conditions.

The survey has shown however that few countries have so far adapted their legal provisions to allow for this kind of health information sharing across borders: only 11% of responding countries reported that they had such legislation in place. It is however even more worrying that only 26% responded that their legal system provided for sharing such information between care providers in their own country, a clear example of the fact that slow adaptation of the law is hindering optimal use of eHealth tools.

Access to patient data is however not only important for individual care; it is integral to the emerging concept of health data as a public good. The potential of the longitudinal health record for clinical research is immense and has been well documented by scientists (46, 47), but is generally underrecognized in law and policy (70). The experience of social networking sites such as PatientsLikeMe demonstrates however that patients are ready and willing to share with each other so that other people can benefit from their experiences. As the OECD notes in their 2010 report on challenges in health care: "we need to look beyond a definition of patient doctor interaction as purely information-seeking and see patients and their information as a core element of future health research" (14).

- Legislation should be adopted to ensure that patient data can be shared safely for direct patient care.

- Legislation should be adopted to support a suitable balance between accessibility of data and the levels of privacy patients wish to maintain.

- Patients should be empowered to make their data available for secondary research through easily understandable and applicable privacy legislation.

- Legislation should be adopted to facilitate appropriate use of EHRs for research.

It is clear that it will require not only legislative change specifically addressing privacy and sharing of EHRs, but also the adoption of new tools and related legislation to embed the use of EHRs in health systems. In countries with well established paper record systems the digitization of records and adoption of new information governance models to facilitate appropriate sharing of records is well underway. However, in countries where the paper record systems are less well developed and where significant variation exists between rural and urban areas, the intrtoduction of new technologies such as Unique Identifiers will have a significant impact on the potential to share records and make data work for the good of public health. Thus the European initiative to adopt common standards for electronic identification to ensure that patients can be identified and their data in any EU country, as well as the ambitious Indian Unique Identifier initiative (Aadhaar) will both have a significant impact in fostering an environment which will allow for safer sharing of EHRs.

While it is paramount that patient trust should not be undermined and that privacy must always be maintained in situations where patients want it, it is perhaps time to move away from a paternalistic approach to patient privacy and to use the law to facilitate safe sharing of patient data for research in ways that allow patients to contribute to the ongoing improvement of clinical care when they want to do so. The survey responses discussed here however do not indicate that many countries have started to explore the full capacity of secondary uses of data in EHRs.

Given that privacy of the doctor-patient relationship is at the heart of good health care, and that the EHR is at the heart of good eHealth practice, the question arises: Is privacy legislation at the heart of the EHR? Based on the responses provided by WHO Member States the answer would seem to be 'yes' but only a qualified 'yes'. To date the use of law has not extended much beyond simple privacy protection in many countries, with only a few adopting legislation to facilitate appropriate sharing of EHR data and even fewer adopting legislation to support patients' more nuanced interests in data such as a right to correction or deletion. It may be suggested therefore that at present the legislative heart is beating weakly and is failing to pump the power of law to the wider reaches of EHR use to enable health care systems to gain the full benefit of a shareable, accessible, and protected EHR.

5 References

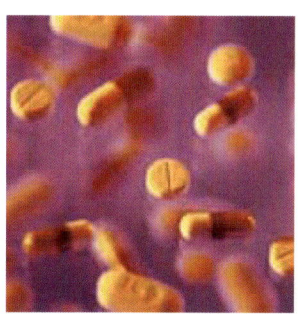

1. Higgins G. The history of confidentiality in medicine: the physician-patient relationship. *Canadian Family Physician*, 1989, 35:921–926.
2. De George RT. *The ethics of information technology and business*. Oxford, Blackwell, 2003.
3. Lyon D. *Surveillance studies: an overview*. Cambridge, Polity Press, 2007.
4. Feng J-X and Hughes J. Analyzing privacy and security issues in the Information Age. *WSEAS Transactions on Information Science and Applications*, 2009, 6(1):220–223.
5. Lu Y. Privacy and data privacy issues in contemporary China. *Ethics and Information Technology*, 2005, 7:7–15.
6. Orito Y, Murata K. Privacy protection in Japan: cultural influence on the universal value. *Proceedings of ETHICOMP*, 2005 (CD-ROM).
7. Collste G. Global ICT-ethics: the case of privacy. *Journal of Information, Communication & Ethics in Society*, 2008, 6(1):76–87.
8. Giddens A. *The consequences of modernity*. Cambridge, MA, Polity Press, 1990.
9. Mayfair MHY. Mass media and transnational subjectivity in Shanghai. In: Ginsberg F, Abu-Lughod L, & Larkin B, eds. *Media worlds*. California, University of California Press, 2002.
10. 2009 *Ageing report: economic and budgetary projections for the EU-27 Member States 2008-2060*. Brussels, Directorate-General for Economic and Financial Affairs of the European Commission, 2009 (http://ec.europa.eu/economy_finance/publications/publication14992_en.pdf, accessed 15 December 2011).
11. Alber J, Köhler U. *Health and care in an enlarged Europe*. Luxembourg, European Foundation for the Improvement of Living and Working Conditions, 2004 (http://www.eurofound.europa.eu/publications/htmlfiles/ef03107.html,, accessed 1 December 2011.)
12. *Together for health: a strategic approach for the EU 2008-2013*. White Paper. Brussels, European Commission, 2007, (http://ec.europa.eu/health/ph_overview/Documents/strategy_wp_en.pdf, accessed 1 December 2011).
13. Stroetman V et al. Understanding the role of device level interoperability in promoting health – lessons learnt from the Smart Personal Health Project. *Year Book Medical Informatics*, 2011, 87–92.
14. *Improving health sector efficiency: the role of information and communication technologies*. Organisation for Economic Co-operation and Development, 2010 (http://ec.europa.eu/health/eu_world/docs/oecd_ict_en.pdf, accessed 1 December 2011).

15. Policy Engagement Network. *Electronic health privacy and security in developing countries and humanitarian operations.* London School of Economics and Political Science, 2010 (http://www.lse.ac.uk/collections/informationSystems/research/policyEngagement/ehealthPrivacy.pdf, accessed 1 December 2011).
16. Nagral A. Privacy in public hospitals. *Indian Journal of Medical Ethics*, 1995, 3(1):22.
17. Brogen S et al. Knowledge and attitudes of doctors on medical ethics in a teaching hospital. *Indian Journal of Medical Ethics*, 2009, 6(4):194–197.
18. Tetali S. The importance of patient privacy during a clinical examination. *Indian Journal of Medical Ethics*, 2007, 4(2):66.
19. Feder L. Cell-phone medicine brings care to patients in developing nations. *Health Affairs*, 2010, 29(2):259–263.
20. Goodman K, Miller R. Ethics and health informatics: users, standards, and outcomes. In: Shortliffe E, Cimino JJ, eds. *Biomedical Informatics*. New York, Springer Verlag, 2006.
21. Bath P. Informatics: current issues and challenges. *Journal of Information Science*, 2008, 34:501.
22. McClanahan K. Balancing good intentions: protecting the privacy of electronic health information. *Bulletin of Science, Technology & Society*, 2008, 28(1): 69–79.
23. Tang P, Lansk D. The missing link: bridging the patient–provider health information gap. *Health Affairs*, 2005, 24(5):1290–1295.
24. Safran C. Electronic medical records: a decade of experience. *Journal of the American Medical Association*, 2001, 285(13):1766.
25. *"I Swear by Apollo Physician...": Greek medicine from the Gods to Galen.* As translated by Michael North for the National Library of Medicine. Available at http://www.nlm.nih.gov/hmd/greek/greek_oath.html (accessed 1 December 2011).
26. Miles SH. *The Hippocratic Oath and the ethics of medicine.* Oxford, Oxford University Press, 2005.
27. Edelstein L. *The Hippocratic Oath: text, translation and interpretation.* Baltimore, John Hopkins Press, 1943.
28. *Principles of medical ethics.* American Medical Association, 1980 (http://www.ama-assn.org/ama/pub/physician-resources/medical-ethics/code-medical-ethics/principles-medical-ethics, accessed 1 December 2011).
29. Olivari C et al. Breaking patient confidentiality: comparing Chilean and French viewpoints regarding the conditions of its acceptability. *Universitas Psychologica*, 2011, 10(1):13–26.
30. Beauchamp TL, Childress JF. *Principles of biomedical ethics.* 6th edition. New York, Oxford University Press, 2001.
31. Hoffman S, Podgurski A. Finding a cure: the case for regulation and oversight of electronic health record systems. *Harvard Journal of Law and Technology*, 2008, 103:117–119.
32. Kottow MH. Medical confidentiality: an intransigent and absolute obligation. *Journal of Medical Ethics*, 1986, 12:117–122.
33. Rothstein M. The Hippocratic bargain and health information technology. *Journal of Law, Medicine & Ethics*, 2010, 38(1):7–13.
34. Montgomery J. *Health care law.* Oxford, Oxford University Press, 2003.
35. Wafa T. How the lack of prescriptive technical granularity in HIPAA has compromised patient privacy. *Northern Illinois University Law Review*, 2010, 30(3):531–553.
36. ECHR. Z v. Finland (9/1996/627/811).
37. Colak and Tsakiridis v. Germany no. 77140 and 35493/05 (fifth Section) ECHR 2010/2.
38. *Protection of personal data.* European Commission, 2007 (http://ec.europa.eu/justice_home/fsj/privacy/workinggroup/wpdocs/2006_en.htm, accessed 1 December 2011).
39. *Privacy and Human Rights 2006.* An international survey of privacy laws and developments. London, Privacy International, 2007 (https://www.privacyinternational.org/phr, accessed 1 December 2011).
40. Sarabdeen J, Ishak M. E-health data privacy: how far is it protected? *Communications of the International Business Information Management Association*, 2008, 1:110–117.
41. Patrício CM et al. O prontuário eletrônico do paciente no sistema de saúde brasileiro [The electronic patient record in the Brazilian health system: is it a reality for the physicians]? *Scientia Medica* (Porto Alegre), 2011, 21(3):121–131.
42. *The security rule.* U.S. Department of Health & Human Services, 2003 (http://www.hhs.gov/ocr/privacy/hipaa/administrative/securityrule/index.html, accessed 3 December 2011).
43. Scalia J. Concurring in judgment in Supreme Court of the United States NASA v. Nelson 131 S. Ct. 746 (2011).
44. Directive 2011/24/EU on the application of patients' rights in cross-border healthcare.

45. Terry N. What's wrong with health privacy? *Journal of Health & Biomedical Law*, 2009, 5:1–32.
46. Hall M. Property, privacy, and the pursuit of interconnected electronic medical records. *Iowa Law Review*, 2010, 95:631–651.
47. Rodwin M. Patient data: property, privacy & the public interest. *American Journal of Law and Medicine*, 2010, 586–611.
48. Evans B. Much ado about data ownership. *Harvard Journal of Law and Technology*, 2011 (in press), available at: http://ssrn.com/abstract=1857986 (accessed 3 December 2011).
49. Calcutt D et al. *Report of the committee on privacy and related matters*. London, Her Majesty's Stationery Office, 1990.
50. Markesinis B et al. *Concerns and ideas about the developing English Law of Privacy (and how knowledge of foreign law might be of help)*. A research project undertaken by the Institute of Global Law. Available at: http://www.ucl.ac.uk/laws/global_law/publications/institute/docs/privacy_100804.pdf (accessed 3 December 2011).
51. *Information governance*. National Health Service. See: http://www.connectingforhealth.nhs.uk/systemsandservices/infogov (accessed 15 December 2011).
52. Simon S et al. Patients' attitudes toward electronic health information exchange: qualitative study. *Journal Medical Internet Research*, 2009,11(3):e30.
53. Ashish K et al. Use of electronic health records in U.S. hospitals. *New England Journal of Medicine*, 2009, 360:1628–1638.
54. DesRoches CM. Electronic health records in ambulatory care - a national survey of physicians. *New England Journal of Medicine*, 2008, 359(1):50–60.
55. *Towards the establishment of a European eHealth research area*. European Commission, 2007 (http://www.ehealth-era.org/documents/2007ehealth-era-countries.pdf, accessed 3 December 2011).
56. Legido-Quigley H et al. Patient mobility in the European Union. *British Medical Journal*, 2007, 334(7586):188–190.
57. *The three ages of eHealth*. A Briefing Paper. European Health Telematics Association (EHTEL), 2010 (http://www.ehtel.org/references-files/ehtel-briefing-papers-pdf/the-three-ages-of-ehealth-briefing-paper-v-public.pdf, (accessed 3 December 2011).
58. Wilson P. Balancing Opportunities and Ethics. In: Rigby M, Roberts J, Thick M eds. *Taking health telematics safely into the twenty first century*. Oxford, Radcliffe Medical Press, 2000.
59. Wilson P. The electronic health record - a new challenge for privacy and confidentiality. *Medicine & Biomedical Ethics*, 1999, 4(2).
60. Sellars C, Easey A. Electronic health records: data protection issues in Europe. In: *BNA International World Data Protection Report*. McDermott, Will & Emery, 2008.
61. Allaert F. Le dossier médical personnel du patient : réflexions sur le portail d'accès unique et le masquage du dossier. *IRBM*, 2009, 30:114–118.
62. Hoffman S, Podgurski A. *Balancing privacy, autonomy and scientific needs in electronic health records*. Case Research Paper Series in Legal Studies. Working Paper 2011, available at: http://papers.ssrn.com/sol3/papers.cfm?abstract_id=1923187 (accessed 3 December 2011).
63. Section 164.512(b) of title 45 Code of Federal Regulations, United States of America.
64. Sections 164.501 and 164.512(i) of title 4 Code of Federal Regulations, United States of America.
65. Sections 164.514(b)(2)(i) of title 4 Code of Federal Regulations, United States of America.
66. Evans B. *Waiving your privacy goodbye: privacy waivers and the HITECH Act's regulated price for sale of health data to researchers*. University of Houston/Health Law & Policy Institute Working Paper No. 2010-A-22, 2010 http://ssrn.com/abstract=1660582, accessed 3 December 2011).
67. *Connecting Americans to their health-care: final report of the Working Group on Policies for Electronic Information Sharing between Doctors and Patients*. Markle Foundation, 2004 www.connectingforhealth.org/resources/wg_eis_final_report_0704.pdf, accessed 3 December 2011).
68. Wynia M, Dunn K. Physicians using personal health records. *J Law Med Ethics*, 2010, 38:64–73.
69. Angst C. Protect my privacy or support the common-good? Ethical questions about electronic health information exchanges. *Journal of Business Ethics*, 2009, 90:169–178.
70. Francis LP. The physician-patient relationship and a national health information network. *Journal of Law, Medicine & Ethics*, 2010, 38(1):36–49.

Appendix 1. Methodology of the second global survey on eHealth

Purpose

The World Health Organization's eHealth resolution WHA 58.28 was adopted in 2005 and focused on strengthening health systems in countries through the use of eHealth (1); building public-private partnerships in ICT development and deployment for health; supporting capacity building for the application of eHealth in Member States; and the development and adoption of standards. Success in these areas is predicated on a fifth strategic direction: monitoring, documenting and analysing trends and developments in eHealth and publishing the results to promote better understanding. In direct response to the eHealth resolution, the Global Observatory for eHealth (GOe) was established to monitor and analyse the evolution of eHealth in countries and to support national planning through the provision of strategic information.

The GOe's first objective was to undertake a global survey on eHealth to determine a series of benchmarks at national, regional and global levels in the adoption of the necessary foundation actions to support the growth of eHealth. The aim was to provide governments with data that could be used as benchmarks for their own development as well as a way to compare their own progress with that of other Member States. The survey is part of the mandate defined during the GOe's inception – to provide Member States with reliable information and guidance on best practices, policies and standards in eHealth.

The second global survey on eHealth was conducted in late 2009 and was designed to build upon the knowledge base generated by the first survey. While the first survey conducted in 2005 was more general and primarily asked high-level questions at the national level, the 2009 survey was thematically designed and presented more detailed questions. The thematic design of the survey has provided the GOe with a rich source of data that is being used to create a series of eight publications – *The Global Observatory for eHealth Series* – due for publication during 2010 and 2011.

Each publication in the series is primarily targeted to ministries of health, ministries of information technology, ministries of telecommunications, academics, researchers, eHealth professionals, nongovernmental organizations involved in eHealth, donors, and private sector partners.

Survey implementation

Based on the experience of the first global survey, the GOe benefited from many of the lessons learned in creating the second survey, disseminating the instrument in digital format, working with WHO regional offices and Member States to encourage survey completion, as well as processing the data and analysing the results.

Survey instrument

The instrument focused on issues relating to processes and outcomes in key eHealth areas. Objectives for the survey were to identify and analyse trends in the:

- uptake of eHealth foundation policies and strategies, building on the 2005 results;
- deployment of mHealth initiatives in countries;
- application of telemedicine solutions;
- adoption of eLearning for health professionals and students;
- collection, processing and transfer of patient information;
- development of legal and ethical frameworks for patient information in digital format;
- action concerning online child safety, Internet pharmacies, health information on the Internet, and spam; and
- governance and organization of eHealth in countries.

Table A1 shows the seven themes of the survey.

Theme	Action
mHealth	Identify the diverse ways mobile devices are being used for health around the world and the effectiveness of these approaches. Highlight the most important obstacles to implementing mHealth solutions. Consider whether mHealth can overcome the digital divide.
Telemedicine	Identify and review the most frequently used telemedicine approaches across the globe as well as emerging and innovative solutions. Propose necessary actions to be taken to encourage the global growth and acceptance of telemedicine, and particularly in developing countries.
Management of patient information	Describe the issues relating to the management of patient information at three levels – local health care facility, regional/district, national levels. Analyse the trends in transition from paper to digital records. Identify actions to be taken in countries to increase the uptake of digital patient records.
Legal and ethical frameworks for eHealth	Review the trends in the introduction of legislation to protect personally identifiable data and health-related data in digital format as well as the right to access and control one's own record. Identify and analyse the control of online pharmacies by Member States. Review government action to provide for child safety on the Internet.
eHealth policies – a systematic review	Identify the uptake of eHealth policies across the globe and analyse by WHO region as well as World Bank income groups to establish possible trends. Systematically review the content and structure of existing strategies highlighting strengths and weaknesses. Propose model approaches for the development of eHealth policies including scope and content.
eHealth foundation actions	Review trends in the uptake of foundation actions to support eHealth at the national level including: eGovernment, eHealth, ICT procurement, funding approaches, capacity building for eHealth, and multilingual communications.
eLearning	Analyse the extent of use and effectiveness of eLearning for the health sciences for students and health professionals.
eHealth country profiles	Presentation of all participating Member States eHealth data aggregated by country to act as ready reference of the state of eHealth development according to selected indicators.

Table A1. Survey themes

Survey development

The survey instrument was developed by the GOe with broad consultation and input from eHealth. Planning for the 2009 global survey started in 2008 with the review of the 2005/2006 survey results, instrument and feedback from participating countries. One of the constraints identified in the first survey was on the management of data and its availability for compilation and analysis. In order to facilitate data collection and management, Data Collector (DataCol)[7] was used to make the survey instrument available online therefore streamlining the collection and processing of data.

A set of questions was developed and circulated in the first quarter of 2009 for comments to selected partners in all regions through virtual teleconferences. The range of partners included those from government, WHO regional and country offices, collaborating centres and professional associations. Over 50 experts worldwide were involved in the process. Collaborative efforts extended to other WHO programmes as well as international organizations, such as the International Telecommunications Union (ITU) and Organisation for Economic Co-Operation and Development (OECD). An online forum to discuss the survey instrument and survey process was developed and hosted by the Institute for Triple Helix Innovation based at the University of Hawaii at Manoa in the United States of America.[8]

A draft questionnaire was developed and posted online for review by the partners and was pilot tested in March 2009 in five countries: Canada, Lebanon, Norway, Philippines, and Thailand. The final version of the survey instrument was enhanced based on the comments and observations received from the pilot testing. In order to encourage countries to respond, the survey questions, instructions and data entry procedures were translated into all WHO official languages plus Portuguese.

Data Collector

Data Collector, DataCol, is a web-based tool that simplifies online form creation for data collection and management and is designed, developed and supported by WHO. The collected data are stored in a SQL database maintained by WHO database administrators, and can be exported as a Microsoft Excel file for further analysis using other statistical software.

This is the first time that DataCol has been used as the primary method of implementing an online survey of over 40 pages of text and questions. Significant preparation and testing was required to ensure that the system was robust and able to accommodate the data entry process from around the world, as well as the volume of data entered and stored online.

The various language versions of the survey instrument and supporting documentation were entered into DataCol by language. In addition, individual country login names and passwords were assigned to ensure that only one entry was submitted per country rather than multiple entries. Country coordinators were responsible for completing the forms after obtaining agreement from the expert informant group.

---

[7] Web-based tool for online creation of forms in surveys developed by WHO.
[8] http://www.triplehelixinstitute.org

Preparation to launch the survey

One of the most important tasks in executing an international survey is to build a network of partners at the regional level who can liaise directly with countries. Due to differing priorities across WHO regions, not all regional offices have staff whose responsibilities included eHealth activities. For this reason many regional offices had to assign staff to assist in coordinating the survey process with countries in their respective region. Instructions for the survey procedures were circulated and were followed by a series of teleconferences.

One significant outcome during the survey implementation was the development of strong and productive working relationships with regional counterparts, without whom it would not have been possible to successfully undertake such a task. The success of the survey implementation can also be attributed to the assistance of regional and national office colleagues who worked directly with national counterparts in completing the questionnaire. Figure A1 shows the steps involved in survey process.

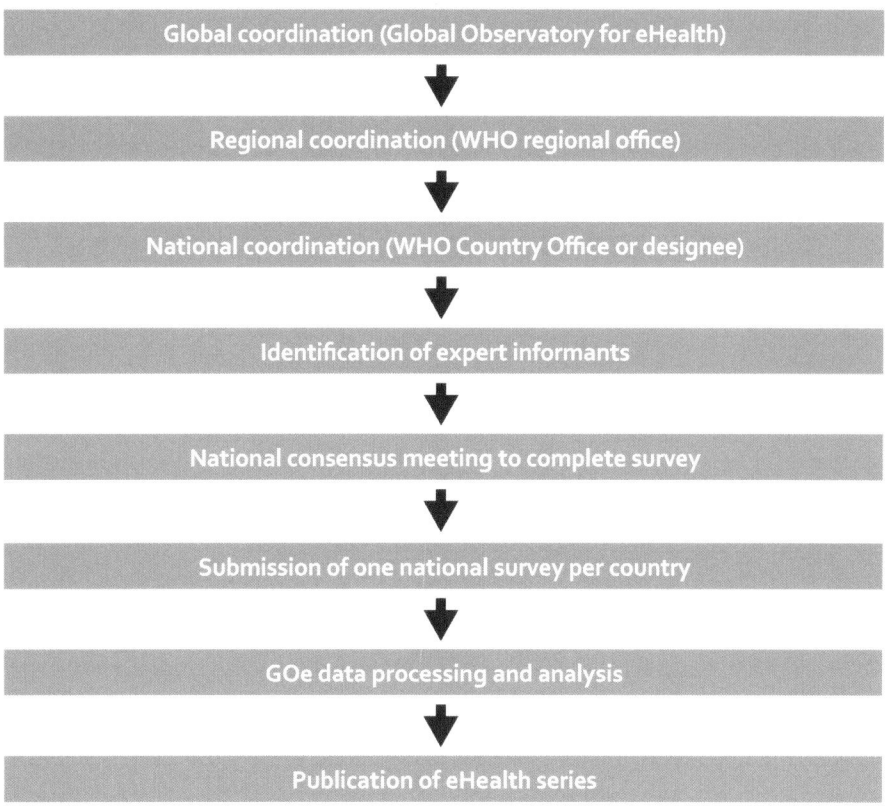

Figure A1. GOe survey and report process

Survey

The survey was launched on 15 June 2009, and due to the high level of interest, did not close until 15 December 2009. Regional focal points worked to encourage Member States to participate. In some cases this was easy; in others it required extensive discussions, not all of which were successful in achieving participation. Conducting a global survey is like conducting a campaign: the purpose and rewards of participation have to be conveyed to national coordinators and then to survey expert informants. It is important to build momentum and to maintain enthusiasm.

At the national level coordinators managed the task. Their responsibilities included finding experts in all of the areas addressed by the survey, and organizing and hosting a full-day meeting where the survey could be collectively completed by the entire group. The number of expert informants, per country, ranged from 5 to 15. The survey process helps build the GOe network of informants around the globe and now consists of over 800 eHealth experts.

Limitations

Member States were limited to one response per country; thus, the expert informants were required to come up with a single response for each question that was most representative of the country as a whole. Coming to a consensus could be difficult in cases where the situation varies widely within the country, or where there were significant differences in opinion. The survey does not attempt to measure localized eHealth activity at the subnational level.

The survey responses were based on self-reporting by the expert informant group for each participating Member State. Although survey administrators were given detailed instructions to maintain consistency, there was significant variation across Member States in the quality and level of detail in the responses, particularly for the descriptive, open-ended questions. While survey responses were checked for consistency and accuracy, it was not possible to verify the responses for every question.

The scope of the survey was broad, and survey questions covered diverse areas of eHealth – from policy issues and legal frameworks to specific types of eHealth initiatives being conducted in-country. Every effort was made to select the best national experts to complete the instrument; however, it is not possible to determine whether the focus groups had the collective eHealth knowledge to answer each question. While the survey was circulated with a set of detailed instructions and terminological definitions, there is no guarantee that these were used when responding.

Data processing

On receipt of the completed questionnaires, all non-English responses were translated into English. Survey responses were checked for consistency and other errors, and countries were contacted for follow-up to ensure accurate reporting of results. Data were exported from DataCol in Microsoft Excel format and the data analysis was performed using R statistical programming language.[9]

Data were analysed by thematic section. For closed-ended questions, percentages were computed for each possible response to obtain the global level results. In addition, the data were aggregated and analysed by WHO region and World Bank income group to see trends by region and by income level. Preliminary analysis based on aggregation by ICT Development Index showed similar results as for World Bank income group (2). This is due to the high correlation between ICT Development Index and GDP per capita (Spearman $\rho=0.93$, $p=10\text{-}16$). Therefore, these results were not included in this report. Cross-question analysis was performed where two or more questions were thought to be related, and the results were probed in greater depth as warranted. External health and technology indicators, such as mobile phone penetration, were introduced into the analysis for comparison purposes where relevant.

Results from the current survey were compared to those from the previous survey wherever possible; however, as the subject matter covered by the 2009 survey was considerably broader, and the survey questions were worded somewhat differently, there was little scope for this sort of analysis. In addition, the percentages were often not directly comparable, particularly at the regional level, as the sets of responding countries were different, and the expert informants in each iteration of the survey were also different.

Table A2 shows the advantages and disadvantages of the groupings used in the survey.

Country grouping	Advantages	Disadvantages
WHO region	WHO regional approach integrated into WHO strategic analysis and planning, and operational action.	Limited country commonality from an economic, health care, or ethnic perspective. Less useful for other agencies or institutions wishing to interpret or act on GOe data.
World Bank income group	Clear economic definition based on GNI per capita. Consistent application of criteria across all countries. Simple four-level scale.	Does not account for income disparity, ongoing armed conflicts, health of the population, or population age.

Table A2. Advantages and disadvantages of the country groupings

---

9   See for more information http://www.r-project.org

Response rate

The "Legal frameworks for eHealth" module of the survey, which this publication is based on, was completed by a total of 113 countries (59% of all WHO Member States). Figure A2 shows the distribution of the responding Member States for this module of the survey. Tables A3 and A4 show the distribution of the responding countries by WHO region and World Bank income group.

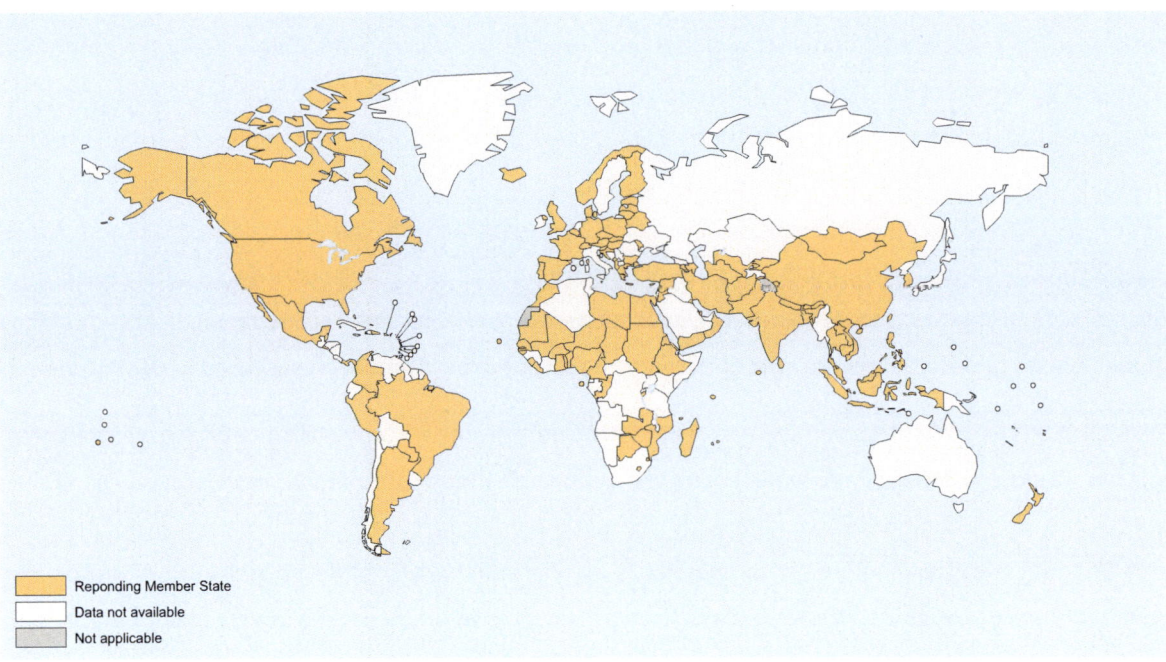

Figure A2. Responding Member States

Response rate by WHO region

Administratively WHO is made up of six geographical regions, which are quite heterogeneous: Member States differ with respect to size, economy, and health care challenges. Nevertheless, it is still important to present high-level eHealth analyses at the regional level as this reflects the organizational structure and operational framework of WHO.

A breakdown by WHO regional responses is presented in Table A3. It shows considerable variation ranging from 34% for the Americas to 73% for the South-East Asia Region. Numerous Member States, particularly those in the Region of the Americas, indicated that they would not be able to participate in the 2009 survey due to resources being diverted to prepare and respond to the H1N1 pandemic or due to other urgent public health issues such as conflict situations. The Western Pacific Region has many small island Member States of which only a few responded to the survey, yielding a response rate of 48% for the region. The response rates for the Eastern Mediterranean, African, and European Regions were over 60%. This was particularly encouraging for regions consisting of a large number of Member States such as the African and European Regions. Results from regions with low response rates should be interpreted with care as they may not be representative of the entire region.

	WHO region					
	African	Americas	South-East Asia	European	Eastern Mediterranean	Western Pacific
Total number of countries	46	35	11	53	21	27
No. of responding countries	29	12	8	36	14	13
Response rate	63%	34%	73%	68%	67%	48%

Table A3. Response rate by WHO region

For the South-East Asia Region, although the number of responding countries was the lowest, the response rate was the highest since the region consists of a total of 11 Member States. Self-selection of the sample often occurs in surveys of this nature, where responding countries are more likely to have a high level of interest and/or activity in eHealth. Table A4 shows that response rates in low and lower-middle income brackets were high. Past surveys have shown that countries in these groups generally have less eHealth activity in comparison to high and upper middle-income brackets. Thus, in some cases, Member States participating in the survey may reflect a commitment to moving forward with eHealth.

Response rate by World Bank income group

The World Bank classifies all economies with a population greater than 30 000 into four income groups based on gross national income (GNI) per capita. The classification is as follows: low income (US$ 975 or less), lower-middle income (US$ 976–3855), upper-middle income (US$ 3856–11 905), and high income (US$ 11 906 or more). These income groups are a convenient and practical basis for analysis, enabling a review of trends in the survey results based on income level. Classification by income does not correspond exactly to level of development; however, low and middle-income countries are sometimes referred to as 'developing' economies and high-income countries as 'developed', for convenience.

Table A4 shows the survey response rate by World Bank income group. Low-income countries had the highest response rate (70%), closely followed by high-income countries (63%). In terms of raw numbers, the distribution of responding countries was remarkably even, with 30 to 31 countries responding from the high-income, lower-middle income, and low-income groups, and a slightly lower number of countries from the upper-middle income group.

	World Bank income group			
	High income	Upper-middle income	Lower-middle income	Low income
Total no. countries	49	44	53	43
No. of responding countries	31	21	30	30
Response rate	63%	48%	57%	70%

Table A4. Response rate by World Bank income group

References

1. Resolution WHA 58.28. eHealth. In: Fifty-eighth World Health Assembly, Geneva, [insert dates of meeting]. Geneva, World Health Organization, 2005 (http://apps.who.int/gb/ebwha/pdf_files/WHA58/WHA58_28-en.pdf, accessed 18 May 2011).
2. Measuring the information society – the ICT Development Index. Geneva, International Telecommunications Union, 2009 (http://www.itu.int/ITU-D/ict/publications/idi/2009/index.html, accessed 17 May 2011).